A CREATIVE STEP-BY-STEP GUIDE TO

CONTAINER
GARDENING

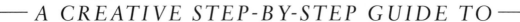

A CREATIVE STEP-BY-STEP GUIDE TO

CONTAINER GARDENING

Author
Sue Phillips
Photographer
Neil Sutherland

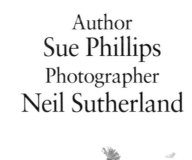

SMITHMARK

CLB 3317
© 1994 CLB Publishing

This edition published in 1995 by SMITHMARK Publishers, Inc.
16 East 32nd Street, New York NY 10016

SMITHMARK books are available for bulk purchase for sales promotion and premium use.
For details write or call the manager of special sales, SMITHMARK Publishers, Inc. 16 East
32nd Street, New York, NY 10016; (212) 532-6600

Produced by CLB Publishing, Godalming Business Centre, Woolsack Way,
Godalming, Surrey, UK

ISBN 0-8317-7790-7

Printed in Singapore
10 9 8 7 6 5 4 3

Credits

Edited and designed: Ideas into Print
Photographs: Neil Sutherland
Photographic location: Russell's Garden Center, Sussex
Typesetting: Ideas into Print and Ash Setting and Printing
Production Director: Gerald Hughes
Production: Ruth Arthur, Sally Connolly, Neil Randles

THE AUTHOR

Sue Phillips began gardening at the age of four, encouraged
by her grandfather, and had her first greenhouse at eleven,
where she grew a collection of cacti and propagated all
sorts of plants. After leaving school, she worked for a year
on a general nursery before studying horticulture at
Hadlow College of Agriculture & Horticulture, Kent for
three years. For the next five years, she was co-owner and
manager of a nursery in Cambridgeshire, before joining a
leading garden products company as Gardens Adviser.
This involved answering gardening queries, handling
complaints, writing articles and press releases, speaking at
gardening events and broadcasting for local radio. In 1984,
she turned freelance and since then she has contributed
regularly to various gardening and general interest
magazines and has appeared often on radio and TV
programs. She is the author of seven published books. She
lives in a very windy village on the south coast of England
near Chichester and has a very intensively cultivated
quarter-acre cottage garden on solid clay, plus a vegetable
garden next door, which she looks after with help from her
husband and hindrance from a Persian cat.

THE PHOTOGRAPHER

Neil Sutherland has more than 25 years experience in a
wide range of photographic fields, including still-life,
portraiture, reportage, natural history, cookery, landscape
and travel. His work has been published in countless books
and magazines throughout the world.

Half-title page: Primroses adorn the head of David.
Title page: Planning and planting up a windowbox.
Copyright page: Terracotta pots to inspire the gardener.

CONTENTS

CONTAINERS - THE GROW ANYWHERE GARDEN

Using pots, tubs and troughs in the garden, you can grow what you like, where you like. You can move containers of plants around in much the same way as you might rearrange the furniture indoors and, what is more, you can even take them with you when you move house. Containers provide instant effect in the garden, as you can plant them up with a tremendous variety of shrubs, perennials, climbers, rock plants and annuals while the plants are in flower. Use containers to create pools of color on the patio, by the front or back door, by a seat, or wherever you need them all round the garden.

Containers are available in a wide range of materials and an even larger range of styles. There is no reason why you should not use a mixture of different types of containers all round the garden, although if you are making a group in a distinct area, such as the patio, it generally looks best to keep to one kind so they look like a 'set'. Some people choose containers to match the style of their house, garden or planting scheme. Others recycle 'finds', such as old baskets, or make their own 'one-off' containers. When it comes to choosing plants for containers, you might suppose that any plants sold in pots will grow in containers long-term, but this is not always the case. Some plants only tolerate containers when young, while naturally large trees and shrubs soon become potbound. But that still leaves the vast majority of plants as potential candidates, from traditional bedding plants, newly fashionable half-hardy annuals, low-maintenance mini-shrubs, grasses, alpines and heathers - and much more. You will find plenty of ideas on the following pages.

Left: Flowers and vegetables flourish in a wooden trough. Right: An oak barrel hosts a dwarf rhododendron.

Choosing containers

Concrete tubs are long-lasting and generally quite frost-resistant, which makes them ideal for all-year-round plantings. Keep the outside clean by scrubbing with a stiff brush when necessary.

Good-quality plastic and other synthetic containers are long-lasting, resistant to cracking in winter and easy to wipe clean. Cheap plastics discolor, become brittle in sunlight and soon need replacing.

Traditional wire hanging baskets need lining before they can hold a planting mixture. Water them daily in summer - if they dry out, they are difficult to rewet. Plant the sides and base, as well as the top, for a stunning result.

Wooden containers have a natural look and are available as tubs, troughs or half-barrels. To prevent them rotting, treat the wood with timber preservative and line the inside with plastic.

Oriental-style glazed pots are good value - often far cheaper than similar terracotta pots. They are claimed to be frost resistant, so shouldn't crack if left outdoors in winter. They often come with matching saucers.

Fiber containers have a peatlike texture, but are actually made from recycled paper. They are cheap to buy, but slowly biodegrade as the material eventually absorbs water from the potting mixture inside.

Terracotta pots have a summery feel, but being porous, dry out much faster in summer than glazed or non-porous ones. Normal clay pots can crack if left outside in winter. Look for frost-proof terracotta.

This reproduction 'hayrack' is treated like half a hanging basket fixed to the wall. Line it with plastic or a liner designed for this type of container and plant through the sides, base and top for a brilliant display.

Modern solid-sided hanging baskets do not dry out as quickly as the traditional wire ones and do not need lining, but you can only plant the top. They are available as both round baskets to hang up and half baskets to go on a wall.

Crocking and liner options

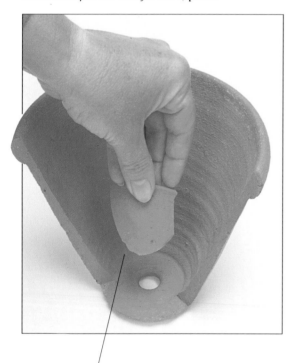

Above: *Woodlice, earthworms and slugs can get into pots through the drainage holes. To prevent this, cover the holes with plastic or the fine metal mesh sold for car bodywork repairs.*

Flowerpots come in two basic types: clay and plastic. Clay pots are porous, so the potting mixture in them dries out quickly due to evaporation through the sides. They are much heavier than plastics and the central drainage hole must be covered with a crock to prevent the soil washing away. Being lighter, plastic pots are the natural choice for roof gardens, hanging baskets and some windowboxes and wall pots. The potting mixture in them is slower to dry out as the sides of the pot are impervious to water, so take care when watering in dull conditions or when the plants are young or sickly and are using less water than usual. Plastic pots are easier to clean and take up less storage space, as they fit tightly inside one another.

Traditional wire hanging baskets must be lined before use. Moss-lined baskets look spectacular, as the wire framework allows you to plant the sides and base of the basket as well as the top, but they drip when watered and dry out quickly. Modern, solid-sided hanging baskets are easier to look after, but you cannot plant the sides. For the best of both worlds, use one of the modern liners inside a traditional basket.

Plastic pots usually have a ring of small drainage holes round the base.

Pieces from broken clay pots are known as 'crocks'.

Above: *Place a large piece of broken clay flowerpot, curved side up, over the drainage hole. Recycle broken clay pots by smashing them with a hammer.*

Clay pots have porous walls.

Plastic pots have thin impervious walls.

Above: *Clay containers have large holes in the base that need covering with crocks to keep the soil in, but allow surplus water to drain out.*

Above: *Plastic pots do not need crocking as soil is unlikely to escape through them, especially the coarser textured peaty potting mixtures.*

Black plastic liners that you cut to shape are disposable and hold water well, but are not very attractive. Cut holes to plant the sides of the basket and make sure that plants soon cover the container.

Reusable coco-fiber looks natural and can be cut to fit. The overlapping panels allow you to plant around the sides of the basket.

Wire baskets must be lined before they will hold soil and plants; they are reusable for many years. Plastic-covered wire frames last longest.

Foam liners hold water well, can be cut to fit and are reusable. The overlapping flanges allow you to push plants through the sides of the basket. Choose natural colors.

Biodegradable, rigid liners are made of a compressed paperlike substance, colored and textured to resemble peat; they hold water well, but you cannot plant through the sides. They rarely last more than a year.

Sphagnum moss in bags is sold especially for lining baskets. It looks very good, but needs a great deal of watering.

Flexible liners with fitted bases are designed for baskets with a particular base size. You can trim them to fit baskets of different heights. Most kinds are reusable.

15

Choosing soils

Visit any garden center, and you will find a wide range of soils, grits, gravels, sands and chippings on sale. What to buy depends very much on what you plan to grow. The basic requirement is for a potting mixture. As a rule, a soil-based potting mixture is preferred for plants that are to be left in the same containers for more than one year, such as alpines and shrubs. This is because soil acts as a 'buffer' and holds more trace elements than peat products. A peat- or coir-based mixture is often preferred for annuals and other bedding plants or bulbs that will only remain in the containers for one growing season. They tend to retain water more than soil-based mixtures, which dry out faster. Plants in a peat or peat substitute mixture will need feeding after four to six weeks.

Right: Use ordinary potting mixture or a special hanging basket formula for hanging baskets and wall pots. If you choose an ordinary mix, peat or coir are usually preferable, as they are lighter in weight.

Ericaceous mix

Hanging basket mix

Above: A soil-based potting mixture is commonly used for plants that will be left in the same container for several years. Being heavier than peaty mixtures, containers that will be left outside in winter are more likely to remain upright in windy weather.

Soil-based potting mixture

Peat-based, multipurpose mix

Coir-based mix

Right: Horticultural, or potting, grit adds weight and air spaces to ordinary potting mixtures. It makes a good growing medium for plants that need particularly well-drained conditions.

Potting grit should contain a mixture of particle sizes, from fine sand to fine grit. Mix one part of grit to four of potting mixture.

Above: Place a layer of coarse grit over the crocks in a trough for herbs or alpines, which need good drainage. Use grit in the base of pots with bulbs left outside through the winter; bulbs will rot if left in wet soil.

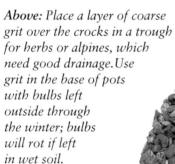

Coarse gravel

Decorative chippings

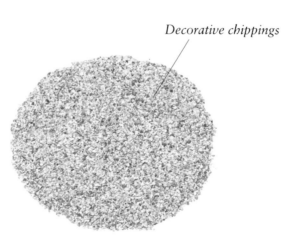

Potting grit

Left: Soil and peat-based potting mixes are the most commonly used. Use ericaceous mix for lime-hating plants. Coir is a 'green' alternative to peat. Hanging basket mixes usually contain water-retaining ingredients.

Right: Grit, chippings and mulching materials are useful optional extras, which can be used for improving drainage in potting mixtures or decorating the surface for certain types of plants grown in containers.

Cocoa shell

Bark chippings

17

Watering and feeding techniques

The secret of successful containers lies in regular feeding and watering. To flower well over a long season, plants need a continuous supply of nutrients - if they go short, the flowering quickly suffers. Check containers daily and water them whenever the potting mix feels dry. In a hot summer, well-filled containers in full bloom may need watering twice a day. Hanging baskets pose the biggest problems. Being high up, you cannot always reach them easily to water. When you do, they drip all over you, and if they dry out badly the water just bounces off the surface without soaking in. Fortunately, there are various products and devices to help with these problems. If you forget to feed regularly, use slow-release fertilizer pills, granules or sachets. If watering is a problem, try self-watering pots or add a water-retaining gel to the soil before planting. If you have several awkward baskets to water, it might be worth investing in a long-handled, hooked, hanging basket watering attachment for your hosepipe, or a device to raise and lower your baskets - buy one for each basket.

Slow-release fertilizer granules

You can mix slow-release fertilizer granules with the potting mixture before planting up a container. To 'top up' later in the season, simply sprinkle more granules over the soil or make a hole with a pencil and push the granules into it. Alternatively, you can buy small bags containing a measured dose of granules. Always read the manufacturer's instructions carefully to see how long you can expect slow-release feeds to last, as individual products vary.

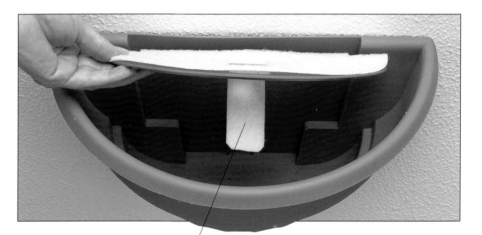

As the soil dries out, the wick draws up water.

Above: This wall basket has a water reservoir built into the base. It stores any surplus water that drains through from the soil above until it is needed.

Water-retaining gel

Mix the dry granules with water and stir to make a thick gel. Combine with the potting mixture. The gel crystals soak up surplus water for later release as the soil dries out.

Right: Terracotta 'water wells' such as this have a wide neck with a spike-shaped base below that is easy to push into the potting mix. Water seeps slowly out through the porous sides so that the soil can absorb it gradually.

Above: Press slow-release fertilizers 'pills' firmly into middle of the soil. The nutrients will slowly escape whenever the potting mix is moist.

Below: Make a watering funnel by cutting a plastic bottle in half. Remove the stopper. Push the neck into the soil so that the funnel is half buried.

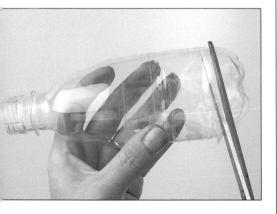

Below: When the funnel is filled, the soil wedged in the neck prevents the water running out too quickly. This method is ideal for hanging baskets.

Above: To lower the basket, release the brake by lifting the basket from below. Support the basket with one hand and let it drop quite quickly. To engage the brake, let the basket slow down as it approaches the right height.

Above: Hose attachments for watering hanging baskets have an on/off switch on the handle, so you only need squirt once the business end is in position. They are invaluable if you have a lot of high baskets.

Below: Water the basket and then raise it back to its original height with a hand supporting it underneath as before. Check that the brake has engaged again before releasing the basket.

Suitable plants for containers

Junipers tolerate the occasional dry spell. Dwarf varieties are the most suitable for containers; this 'Gold Cone' grows to 36in(90cm).

It is surprising how many garden plants thrive in containers. Naturally compact kinds look best and naturally drought-tolerant kinds survive best, although even damp-loving plants thrive in containers if kept well watered. For long-lasting displays, choose flowering plants with a long flowering season and foliage plants with really striking foliage. Traditional container planting schemes made up with annual bedding plants are fine for bright spring and summer color, but nowadays people want container plantings that are a bit different. And now that everyone is busier, the trend is changing towards plants that can stay in the same containers all year round. It can create a more subtle effect, too. You can choose a mixture of small trees, shrubs and ground covering plants, with herbaceous flowers to create a complete potted garden where there is no flowerbed. If you choose a plant that will grow big, it makes sense to give it a good-sized container or it will quickly become potbound. Here are a few ideas.

Potentilla fruticosa is a very good compact shrub for containers in a sunny spot. It tolerates very hot conditions. Named varieties are available with pink, yellow, white or red flowers.

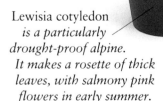

Lewisia cotyledon is a particularly drought-proof alpine. It makes a rosette of thick leaves, with salmony pink flowers in early summer.

Houttuynia cordata 'Chameleon' is a first-class container plant. The shoots do not appear above ground until late spring.

Pinks are free-flowering, compact and survive the occasional drying out. Plants are perennial but shortlived; take cuttings in midsummer to replace old plants every three years.

Ampelopsis brevipedunculata 'Elegans' is an unusual, small perennial climber for a sheltered spot. The leaves are variegated cream, green and pink.

Good container plants

Compact summer bedding plants, e.g. salvia, petunia, french marigold, lobelia, ageratum. Pelargonium, fuchsia, gazania, argyranthemums, felicia (bring indoors for the winter). Winter-flowering pansies, wallflowers, polyanthus, bellis daisies. Spring and summer-flowering bulbs. A selection of herbs, e.g. mint, chervil, parsley. Hostas. Standard trained wisteria. Topiary trained box.

Small trees with good foliage add height to a collection of permanent patio plants. Japanese maples, such as this Acer palmatum 'Ornatum', are very attractive.

Variegated evergreens are particularly valuable in all-year-round planting schemes. Euonymus fortunei varieties, such as this 'Emerald 'n Gold', make neat compact shapes.

Containers are a good way of growing compact shrubs that might not otherwise thrive in your garden soil. This Pieris japonica 'Variegata' needs a slightly shaded, sheltered spot with lime-free soil.

Miniature and patio roses are fine for containers, although other roses do not do very well in them. This one is 'Anna Ford'.

Large-flowered hybrid clematis are excellent in large containers, but give them a good support. This is 'Elsa Spath'.

21

Unsuitable plants for containers

Plants with short flowering seasons, a straggly growth habit, uninteresting foliage, tall gangly stems or only one feature of interest instead of several, generally make unexciting subjects for containers. Some plants need putting into the ground soon after you buy them, as they quickly spoil if they are allowed to dry out at the roots. Other plants are unsuitable for long-term growing in containers because they get too big or grow so vigorously that they soon exhaust the limited amount of potting mixture, even in a large container. This is particularly true of climbing roses, cane fruits and large climbers. However, do not be put off using shade and moisture-loving plants - many of them make good container plants, given the right conditions.

Variegated weeping fig and other tropical foliage plants are easily spoiled in cold and windy, or very sunny conditions. They are much happier if left indoors.

Climbing roses do not do well for long in containers and are much more successful if planted in a permanent soil bed near a wall on which you can properly train their branches.

Some alpines, particularly mossy saxifrages such as this 'Cloth of Gold', scorch badly if they are grown in full sun and allowed to dry out.

Tall herbaceous flowers, such as this lupin, are too top-heavy for a container and lack interest once they have flowered.

Large-flowering houseplants, such as gloxinia, scorch in full sun. Leaves brown if the soil dries out.

22

Raspberries, loganberries and the
blackberry shown here get far too big, soon
exhaust the soil and run out of root room.

This flowering currant has only a
short season of interest in spring.
Choose a shrub with more variety.

Plants to avoid

*Garrya elliptica has brittle roots
that dislike being moved. All
container plants need repotting
every few years to give them
fresh soil, so avoid species that
do not respond well to this, such
as hellebores and euphorbias.
Large trees, including woodland
and forest species, are unsuitable
for containers unless you train
them as bonsai specimens.
Large ornamental trees become
potbound and dry out faster
than you can water them.
Fruit trees are not ideal in pots,
unless grafted onto moderately
dwarfing rootstocks and grown
in large tubs.
Large untidy or fast-growing
shrubs, conifers or flowers soon
outgrow their containers.*

Avoid plants
that cause skin
reactions, such
as rue and
some primulas.
Containers are
often placed
where people
brush against
them.

Plants that grow naturally in
boggy conditions and need sun,
such as this candelabra primula,
quickly die if they dry out.

Huge, fast-growing herbs,
such as angelica, soon
smother other herbs in a tub.

Biennial flowers, such as
sweet williams, have a shorter flowering
time than annuals and are less compact.

Most conifers go brown if
they dry out at the roots and
the foliage remains brown.

23

Container plants for sun

Although most of the plants commonly used in containers grow best in a warm, sheltered spot, they may struggle to survive if conditions are too hot, when they virtually bake. As if intense heat was not enough, containers dry out faster than usual in a very sunny spot, which can mean that plants go short of water. Some kinds of plants are naturally more heat- and drought-tolerant than others. Apart from the examples shown here, as a general guide, look for plants with felty or woolly leaves, silver foliage, and waxy or very narrow or needlelike leaves. The selection need not be dull. There are plenty of exciting and interesting plants you can grow in a 'difficult' hot, dry spot that would not grow anywhere else. The list includes many rock plants, tropical shrubs and climbers that most people could only grow in a conservatory, even in summer, and flowering succulent plants with fat, waxy leaves. You can even use cacti to create interesting and unusual summer container displays.

Sun worshippers

Some alpines, including Lewisia, encrusted saxifrages, Sedum and Sempervivum. Sun-loving shrubs, such as Potentilla, Hebe and Helianthemum. Semi-succulent bedding plants, including Mesembryanthemum and Portulaca. Evergreen herbs.

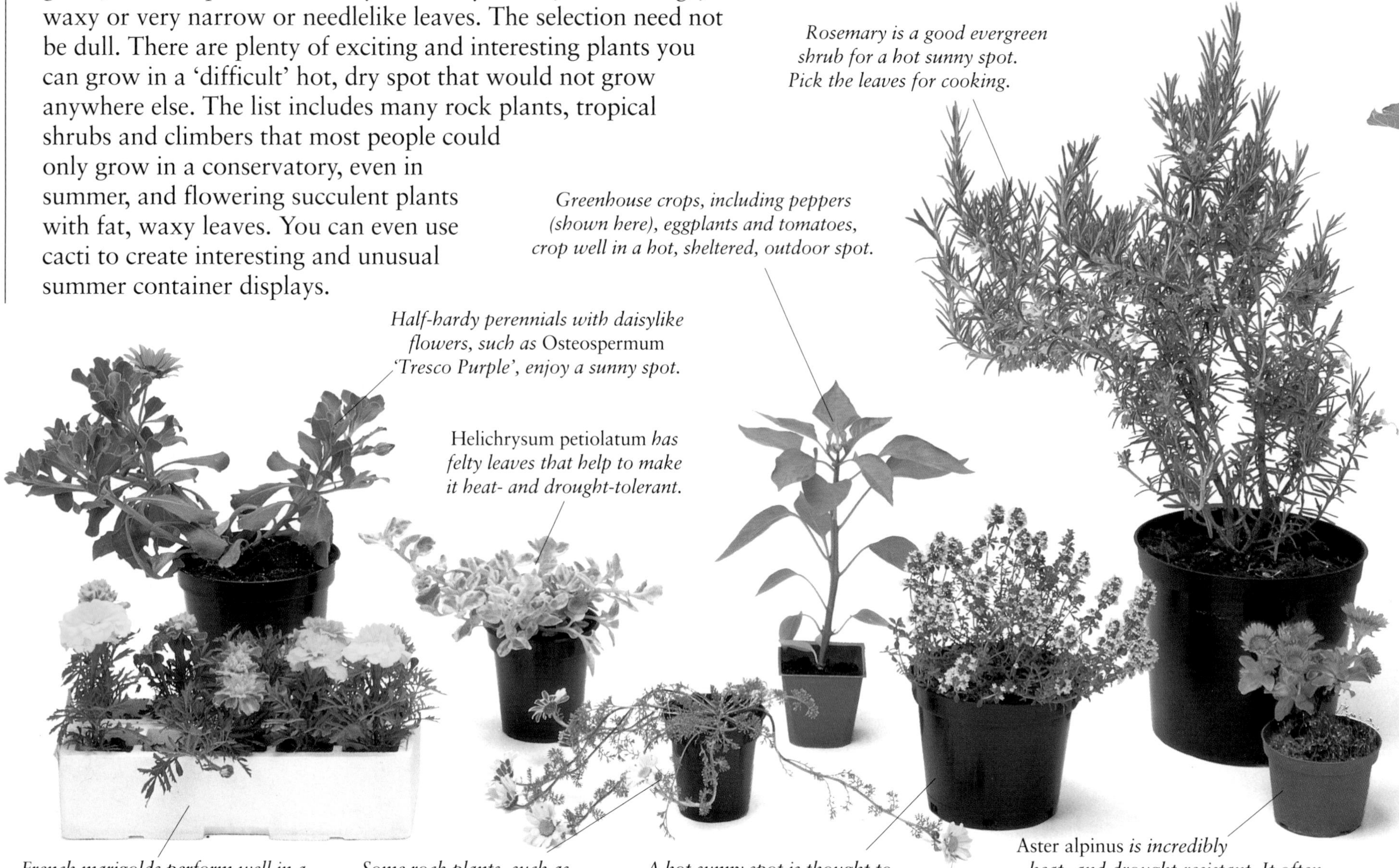

Rosemary is a good evergreen shrub for a hot sunny spot. Pick the leaves for cooking.

Greenhouse crops, including peppers (shown here), eggplants and tomatoes, crop well in a hot, sheltered, outdoor spot.

Half-hardy perennials with daisylike flowers, such as Osteospermum 'Tresco Purple', enjoy a sunny spot.

Helichrysum petiolatum has felty leaves that help to make it heat- and drought-tolerant.

French marigolds perform well in a hot, sunny spot. Keep them well fed and watered, and deadhead regularly.

Some rock plants, such as this Mount Atlas daisy, are adapted to heat and drought.

A hot sunny spot is thought to concentrate the flavor of the leaves of evergreen herbs, such as thyme.

Aster alpinus is incredibly heat- and drought-resistant. It often seeds itself into cracks in walls and paths where nothing else will grow.

In gardens, figs only ripen their fruit in a hot, sunny spot. This outdoor variety is 'Brown Turkey'.

Plants with very narrow, waxy leaves are usually designed that way to withstand heat and drought. This one is a cordyline palm, which has a lovely architectural shape that looks good as a specimen plant in a large container.

Pelargoniums, including the ivy-leaved varieties used in hanging baskets, flower best in a hot spot.

Lampranthus is a succulent that quickly recovers when watered, without impairing flowering.

Hebe pinguifolia 'Pagei' is a compact, drought-resistant shrub with gray leaves and white flowers in summer.

Houseleeks (Sempervivum) are heat- and drought-proof and good for alpine sink gardens and other containers. This is the cobwebbed houseleek (Sempervivum arachnoideum).

Container plants for shade

Containers are traditionally associated with sunny sites, but what do you do if you have a shady corner to decorate? Or a whole garden that is in shade? Fortunately, there are plenty of plants that thrive in this common 'problem' situation. Quite a few plants are fairly easy-going and do well in either sun or partial shade. Others are real shade-lovers and only grow well out of sunlight. This gives you scope either to make the best of a bad job or to take the plunge and create a very 'different' container planting scheme based on true shade-lovers.

A potted shade garden is altogether more subtle than a sunny one, relying on foliage effects and subtle colors for its impact, rather than brash colors. You could install a small fountain, with or without a pond, to add sparkle to the scene and to reflect light back into the darker areas. And take this opportunity to make the most of variegated plants, shapes and interesting containers and backgrounds to see a shade garden at its best. However, do not think that shade gardens need be without color altogether. There are plenty of plants that provide seasonal flowers throughout most of the year.

One potential problem to watch out for in shady gardens - even more so than in sunny ones - is that of slugs and snails. They thrive in the cool, moist shade under plants and find the thin leaves of hostas and toad lilies particularly to their liking. If you do not like using slug pellets, then mulching containers and beds with cocoa-shell seems to deter them.

Hydrangeas do well in containers in a shaded spot, as long as they have plenty of moisture. Leave the dead flowerheads on over winter to protect young shoots, then prune them back to where they join a young branch in spring. This lacecap variety has sterile florets in the center that never open.

Hardy ferns are fantastic foliage plants for shade. Keep them moist. This evergreen one is Phyllitus scolopendrium 'Cristata', the curly hart's tongue fern.

Hostas of all sorts make superb plants for containers and look 'at home' in light shade. They will also grow in sunnier spots, given plenty of water. Slugs love them!

Begonia semperflorens thrives in shade if you delay planting it until it has started flowering.

Specialist growers advertise a range of unusual variegated and curly- or narrow-leaved ivies.

Left: *Hardy ferns and hostas are fashionable and collectable plants for a shady spot. They associate together very well and thrive in containers. Do watch out for watering, as these plants need to be moist at all times.*

Unlike most annuals that need plenty of sun, busy lizzie are useful for providing color in shady areas.

Above: *Fatsia japonica (sometimes called the castor oil plant) has large, striking evergreen leaves and rounded clusters of white flowers in the fall. It associates particularly well with ivies, especially the variegated kinds.*

A dwarf rhododendron makes a good spring display in a large tub. Plant it in a mixture of half ericaceous and half soil-based potting mix.

This alpine strawberry thrives in shade under other plants. The tiny, edible fruits are delicious.

Low, ground-covering perennials with good foliage are useful in all-year-round plantings. This Ajuga reptans 'Braunherz' has shiny purplish black leaves.

27

The outer box will be the depth of the finished container.

1 *Select two strong cardboard boxes that fit one inside the other, leaving a gap between them of about 2in(5cm) all round.*

Making a container from hypertufa

Cement powder

Genuine old stone containers, such as butlers' sinks, are highly sought after by collectors for growing alpines and are very expensive. But there is an alternative; you can now make your own containers from a fake stone mixture called hypertufa. The ingredients are available from any garden center or hardware store. It is cheap, and very versatile. You can cover an old ceramic sink, provided the shiny surface of the sink is first given a coating of outdoor-quality building adhesive. This gives it a rough surface to which the hypertufa can 'key in', otherwise the mixture just slides off. Hypertufa can transform an old container, such as a clay flowerpot, into a stone one, just by giving it a new outer finish. If you have large terracotta pots that have cracked, a coating of hypertufa can hide a repair, where the broken pieces have been joined by a suitable adhesive. You can also make your own free-style containers from scratch using the mixture to cover a foundation made of scrunched up small-mesh chicken wire. Or you could try the cardboard box method, shown here, to make a 'stone' sink or trough.

2 *Cut a piece of board to fit exactly inside the base of the larger, outer box. Nail four wine corks as shown - these will eventually form the drainage holes in the base of the finished container.*

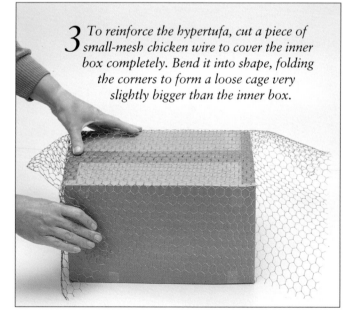

3 *To reinforce the hypertufa, cut a piece of small-mesh chicken wire to cover the inner box completely. Bend it into shape, folding the corners to form a loose cage very slightly bigger than the inner box.*

4 *Slip the smaller box with its wire cover into the larger box. If the wire sticks out at all, bend it down more firmly until it slips in easily.*

5 To make hypertufa, mix equal parts by volume of cement, gritty sand and moss peat or coconut fiber-based peat substitute with enough water to mix to a sloppy paste.

Peat or coir-based substitute

Coarse gritty sand

6 Remove the inner box and wire netting, and trowel enough of the hypertufa mixture over the board base to come to the top of the corks. Do not cover them.

7 Fit the inner box and wire cover into the center and press down firmly, so the wire sinks into the hypertufa and the gap between the boxes is even all round. Fill the gap with hypertufa.

Covering a flowerpot with hypertufa

Start by soaking the flowerpot in water. This is particularly important if you are using a brand new pot. Then, using rubber gloves, press handfuls of the hypertufa all over the surface and stand the pot in a sheltered place to dry slowly. The coarse sand and peat in the mixture will give the pot a rough stonelike texture.

Cover the inside rim of the pot so that when it is planted, the original clay surface will not be visible.

8 Use a piece of wood to ram the mixture well down between the two boxes on each side of the wire mesh so that there are no air pockets. These would turn out as holes in the sides of the finished container.

9 Finish off by roughly rounding and smoothing the exposed surface of the hypertufa - this will form the edges of the container.

Do not worry if the sides of the outer box bow out slightly, this will only improve the finished shape.

The container emerges

Hypertufa takes a long time to dry out, so make the container where you will not need to move it, or put it on top of a firm wooden base that you can lift without touching the sides of the container. Allow six weeks for a large sink or trough made by the cardboard box method to set before you remove the boxes. Do not worry if there are some imperfections, as they add character. Any air pockets left while the hypertufa was in the mold will be apparent as holes in the sides of the container. If they go right through, or can be enlarged to do so, transform them into side planting pockets. Hypertufa continues to dry for a time after the mold is removed. When it is completely dry it turns a pale gray color very similar to stone. If you used coarse textured sand and peat in the mix, it will also have a craggy texture. The longer you leave hypertufa containers outside in the open air, the more weathered and stonelike they become. To speed up the aging process, spray the sides with diluted liquid houseplant feed. This encourages lichens and moss to gradually colonize them, creating the look of a genuine aged stone container.

3 Carefully cut away the cardboard from the sides of the container. Do not hurry or you may pull pieces of hypertufa away with the cardboard. Peel off loose paper shreds with your fingers.

1 After six weeks, gently peel back the sides of the inner cardboard box to check if the hypertufa is 'done'. Even so, it will not be very firm, so treat it gently for several more weeks.

2 Remove the inner box by folding it inwards, then lifting out the base one end at a time. Take your time, as forcing it may damage the container.

4 You can sometimes remove thin slivers of paper on the sides of the container by wetting them and then peeling them off with a knife, or by wire-brushing. They will eventually disappear when the trough has been out in the garden for a while.

A drop of liquid detergent in the water helps to remove scraps of cardboard sticking to the surface.

Use the wire brush to roughen up smooth surfaces.

5 Gently turn the container over to remove the cardboard from the base. Prise the wooden board away from the base. The corks will be left behind in the hypertufa.

6 Drill through the corks to make the drainage holes in the base of the container. This is much safer than trying to drill holes into the hypertufa, which could crumble and split.

7 The finished container is ready for planting, with a sensible number of drainage holes for its size - something genuine old sinks never have. When it is standing in its final position, raise the container on two bricks to allow surplus water to drain away.

Round off any sharp edges with a wire brush.

1 Cover the drainage holes in the base of the container with crocks to stop the soil trickling out through them. Any surplus water can still escape.

Alpines in hypertufa

Any plants that will grow in normal containers will also grow in hypertufa, but stone or hypertufa containers are mostly used for rock plants. All sorts of alpines, dwarf bulbs and drought-tolerant small shrubs are suitable, as long as you only group together plants that share similar soil conditions and cultural requirements. Plants that need particularly well-drained potting mix, such as encrusted saxifrages, armerias, erodiums, sedums, sempervivums and lewisias, do best in a mixture of 1 part grit to 4 parts soil-based potting mix. Less fussy rock plants, such as arabis, aubretia, diascia, small hardy cranesbills, such as *Geranium lancastriense,* and most campanulas are quite happy in soil-based potting mix on its own. Gentians can be grown in containers, but need relatively moisture-retentive soil as they dislike drying out; a half-and-half mixture of peat and soil-based potting soils with a little added grit would be best. (Check plant care labels with gentians as some varieties only grow in lime-free soil). They also like partial shade. In a very shady spot, fill the container with the peat/soil mix and plant ramonda and haberlea or primula species and small hardy ferns, such as *Adiantum pedatum,* the bird's foot fern, and *Adiantum venustum,* the hardy maidenhair fern. They all need rather damper conditions than normal alpines; the soil should never quite dry out. Larger shrubby rock plants for stone or fake stone containers include helianthemum, cistus and hebes: the whipcord hebes have dramatic stringlike foliage, although others have more striking flowers.

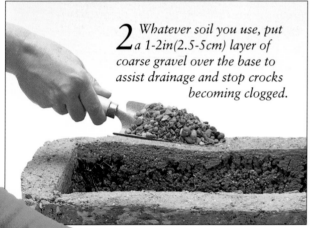

2 Whatever soil you use, put a 1-2in(2.5-5cm) layer of coarse gravel over the base to assist drainage and stop crocks becoming clogged.

Fill the container almost to the rim.

3 For growing alpines in this container, add 1 part of coarse grit to 4 parts of soil-based potting mixture.

Coarse grit

Soil-based potting mix

4 To create an authentic alpine look, bury a craggy chunk of tufa rock in the center of the container as though it were a natural outcrop.

5 This trough has a small hole where an air pocket was left in the mixture. It makes a planting hole for a sedum, pushed through from outside.

6 *Choose alpines that need the same soil and growing conditions. Flowering kinds and those with hillocky shapes and colored foliage make interesting combinations.*

7 *Evergreen plants look interesting in winter when many alpines die down to ground level. In time, they will creep over the sides of the trough and up the tufa chunk.*

Hebe in a hypertufa pot

The hypertufa-covered pot made at the same time as the trough has dried to a stonelike color and would look good standing next to it planted with a compact rockery type shrub. The Hebe franciscana shown here teams well with the rock plants in the trough. Once you have planted the pot, you can also spray the sides with a diluted houseplant feed so that moss and lichen develop to make it look old.

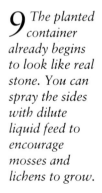

8 *Topdress the finished surface with coarse grit, such as granite chippings. It helps to improve surface drainage and prevents alpines rotting at the neck.*

9 *The planted container already begins to look like real stone. You can spray the sides with dilute liquid feed to encourage mosses and lichens to grow.*

Campanula muralis

Sempervivum *hybrid*

Saxifraga correoevensis

Erodium 'Natasha'

Sedum spurium 'Variegatum'

Rhodohypoxis 'Fred Broome'

Sedum 'Lydium'

An alpine garden

You do not need a rockery to grow alpine plants. They make very good, naturally compact flowering plants for growing in containers of all sorts. But to make them look really 'at home', give them a stone-effect container, such as the textured concrete tub shown here. The majority of commonly available alpines are spring-flowering plants, so a container planted in this way will look its best then. This is why it is a good idea to include a dwarf conifer for all-year-round effect. Many dwarf conifers will turn brown if their roots dry out for any length of time, but the juniper family are much more drought-resistant. The cultivar featured here, 'Blue Star', is particularly suitable for tubs, as it stays naturally small and compact. Other junipers could be grown in a bed in the patio to provide an interesting background for a collection of alpines growing in containers. To add extra 'out-of-season' interest, you could also tuck a few autumn- and spring-flowering bulbs into the tubs, choosing the smallest species so that their flowers remain in proportion to the size of the container and other plants in it. Good examples include spring- and autumn-flowering crocus and the tiny species of narcissi, such as N. asturiensis. These can be taken out of the pot after their leaves die down and stored in a cool, dark place ready to replant in the following year.

4 Knock each plant out of its pot and scoop out a hole large enough to accommodate the rootball. Fill it with potting mix to the same level as the plant occupied in its pot. The conifer makes a good centerpiece. Put this in first and arrange the flowering plants around the edge.

3 Choose a mixture of flowering rock plants and a conifer for foliage interest. Stand the plants on top of the tub, still in their pots, so you can easily rearrange them while you decide where each one looks best.

Primula auricula and Phlox subulata go well together. The phlox makes a low, ground-hugging mat that flowers profusely in spring.

1 Place crocks over the drainage holes in the base and cover the bottom with a 1in(2.5cm) layer of fine gravel. This helps to provide the sharp drainage that rock plants need.

2 Fill the rest of the tub to within 1-2in(2.5-5cm) of the rim with a good-quality, soil-based potting mixture. If the soil looks rather heavy, mix a large potful of grit with it.

Place the dwarf juniper in the center of the pot.

5 If there are any depressions between the plants, trickle a little more potting mix between them so that the surface is level. Leave a 2in(5cm) gap between the soil and the rim of the pot to allow room for a layer of gravel.

6 Add a 0.5in (1.25cm) layer of smooth gravel or coarse stone chippings, tucking it under the plants. This gives a clean finish and also prevents moisture gathering around the necks of plants, which can cause rotting.

Arabis caucasica 'Compinkie'

Sedum spathulifolium 'Cappa Blanca'.

Aubretia 'Blue Cascade' will tumble over the sides of the tub, softening the edges.

Arabis 'Spring Charm' is planted in a group of three, as this makes a more effective splash of color than a single plant.

Juniperus 'Blue Star' stays naturally small, with tightly packed steely-blue foliage that holds its color all year round. It grows to only about 12x12in (30x30cm).

Sedum spathulifolium 'Purpureum'

Phlox subulata

Acaena glauca

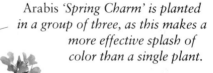

7 Water the plants in with a slow dribble of water to avoid splashing soil up over the gravel. Check the tub every few days in summer and weekly in winter, and water when necessary.

8 The finished container can stand in a sunny spot or in part shade, as long as it is in the sun for at least half the day. Raise it slightly off the ground in winter so that water can easily run away after spells of rain.

35

Planting drought-proof alpines in a pot full of crevices

The more drought-tolerant rock plants, such as sedum, sempervivum and thick-leaved saxifrages, are particularly good for containers in a hot, sunny spot, particularly if the container is likely to dry out quickly, such as this small terracotta strawberry pot. The plants used here for the sides of the pot are all evergreen; *Sedum spurium* 'Variegatum' has red variegated leaves, *Sedum spathulifolium* 'Cappa Blanca', has bluish gray leaves with a powdery 'bloom', and *Sedum spurium* 'Fuldaglut' has red foliage. *Sempervivum pittonii* is a type of houseleek, *Saxifraga* 'Silver Cushion' is pure silver, and *Saxifraga aizoon* 'Baccana' is silver-edged. Most alpines dislike having damp around their 'necks', and rot easily in such conditions. When grown in vertical crevices, as here, moisture runs away quickly, so plants fare better. Choose small plants in tiny pots, as these will be easier to fit into the small planting pockets of the container.

This container is a small version of a strawberry pot. It is really too small for strawberries, but ideal for rock plants, which thrive in the vertical crevices it provides.

1 Most rock plants need well-drained conditions, so a terracotta pot that 'breathes' suits them well. Place a 'crock' over the drainage hole in the bottom of the container and cover the base with 0.5in (1.25cm) of potting grit.

2 Choose a selection of drought-tolerant rock plants in small pots. Go for evergreen types in a good mixture of shapes and leaf colors. These will provide the best all-year-round display.

3 Fill the container to just below the level of the bottom planting pockets, using a good-quality, soil-based potting mixture.

5 *Top the pot up to the rim with more potting mixture, firming it lightly around the roots of the plants in the pockets as you go, so that the soil does not sink when watered.*

Choose a compact trailing plant for the top of the pot so that it cascades down over the sides. This one is Stonecrop (Sedum acre), *which has plenty of small, starlike yellow flowers in summer.*

6 *Tuck a larger spreading plant into the top of the pot; this contrasts well with the rounded shapes of the plants in the pockets. Fill gaps around the edges with more potting mixture.*

7 *Water the plants in using a slow trickle of water so that the potting mixture can absorb it. If you water too quickly, the soil may be washed out of the planting holes.*

As the planting pockets in the container are small, choose plants growing in small pots, as they will be easier to plant.

4 *Knock the plants out of their pots and tuck them into each planting pocket. Squeeze the rootball slightly if necessary so that it fits. Fill the gap between the rootball and the sides of each planting pocket with soil.*

8 *Viewed from above, you can see the shapes the plants make together. Finish off by standing the plant in a matching saucer.*

Creative alpine displays

You can create most attractive displays by grouping together three or five containers of alpines. (Odd numbers always look best). For the best effect, choose similar containers of different sizes, each planted with alpines that grow at roughly the same rate and share similar growing requirements. Alternatively, you could team a sink garden with one large or several smaller pots of alpine plants. Alpine containers also look superb on paving that has ground-hugging alpines planted in the cracks between the slabs. An alpine container garden is an ideal way of housing a collection of interesting plants without taking up a lot of space, but bear in mind that alpines need regular attention to look their best. Water them during dry spells, as the soil should never dry out completely. A layer of grit chippings over the soil surface, tucked in well around the necks of the plants, helps prevent rotting. Remove dead flowers and leaves to prevent plant pests and diseases from gaining a foothold. Every three years or so, remove all the plants, divide or replace them with new ones and replant the container with fresh potting mix and grit.

Above: *This large area of paving has been broken up by a rocky 'outcrop' - four stone butler's sinks amid a rock garden of dwarf conifers for year-round interest.*

Right: *A pair of sinks, raised up so that the larger one is slightly higher, makes a pleasing arrangement, together with pans of smaller plants in typical rock plant surroundings - paving, gravel and a background of small, choice, sun-loving plants.*

Above: Saxifraga oppositifolia
'Splendens' is a ground-hugging
'treasure' that flowers in early spring.
For the rest of the year, the carpet of
tiny, silver-tipped rosettes makes a
useful 'foil' to later flowers. Provide
well-drained soil, but do not allow the
plant to dry out completely.

Like many of the more drought-
tolerant alpines, Lewisia
cotyledon grows very happily
planted vertically into the side of
a wall or, as in this case, a pot.

Left: Lewisia cotyledon hybrids flower in late
spring and early summer. Plants need good
drainage but should not dry right out. Give
them a little extra water when in flower.
After flowering, deadhead and regularly tease
out dead leaves from the base of the rosettes.

39

A versatile windowbox

Windowboxes are on show all the time and so the whole display can be spoiled if one plant is past its best. In this case, it pays to leave plants in their pots and just 'plunge' them into the container up to their rims. You can then lift out and replace individual plants without disturbing the others, leaving a wreath of foliage such as trailing ivy round the edge and altering the flowers in between them as the seasons change. You might choose spring bulbs and polyanthus for instant color in spring, replacing them with annuals, pelargoniums or fuchsias, or perhaps a mixture of culinary and flowering herbs for the summer. In autumn and winter, big cities create their own mild microclimate, allowing you to plant cool-temperature indoor plants, such as cyclamen and exacum, in windowboxes out of doors. (Do not try this unless you have seen other people in your area use the strategy successfully.) It is worth leaving foliage plants in their pots too, so that they can be easily replaced if necessary. As well as ivies, small upright conifer trees and many houseplants (such as asparagus fern) can be used as temporary foliage plants for windowboxes. To look after a windowbox display like this, feed and water the plants regularly. Check the potting mix daily in summer and in windy weather, when they are liable to dry out more rapidly. And keep the soil around the pots moist; as well as helping to keep the plants watered, this creates a humid pocket of air around the plants, which they enjoy.

3 Place the plants, in their pots, into the box. In this formal, symmetrical display, trails of ivy cascade over the sides and flowering plants are grouped in the center.

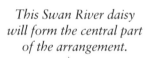

This Swan River daisy will form the central part of the arrangement.

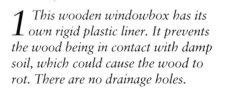

1 This wooden windowbox has its own rigid plastic liner. It prevents the wood being in contact with damp soil, which could cause the wood to rot. There are no drainage holes.

2 Arrange the plants in front of the windowbox. Place 1in(2.5cm) of soilless potting mix in the plastic liner and make a small depression for each pot to stand in.

Ringing the changes

Here, just the Brachycome *and two of the ageratums have been lifted out of the middle of the display and replaced with a tuberous-rooted begonia to show the effect that a small change has on the arrangement.*

4 Fill the space between the pots with more potting mix. This helps to keep the pots in place and retains moisture, acting as a reserve from which the plants can draw as needed.

5 It is easy to lift out fading plants and replace them with fresh ones. Experiment with new 'looks' or alter the composition for a change.

Ageratum

Pelargonium

Swan River daisy (Brachycome)

Trailing ivy

Wonderful windowboxes

Windowboxes must look their best all the time, so they need careful planning and regular replanting. They are normally planted with seasonal flowers and although it means more work, a series of fresh displays looks much more interesting in such a highly visible situation. Choose pot-grown plants already in flower, as they give an instant effect. The most suitable plants for windowboxes are the compact kinds that flower continuously over a fairly long season. You can mix together annuals as you would in normal containers; herbs make another good summer display. Evergreens, such as dwarf conifers or ivies, can be used temporarily as foliage to accompany flowering plants in windowboxes, but do not leave them in for more than a year, as they soon grow too large. Tip out windowboxes every year in spring, just before planting summer bedding, and refill them with fresh potting mix. This is the time to trim or replace overgrown foliage plants.

Left: *An all-year-round framework of dwarf conifers and ivies is teamed with a compact, berrying, evergreen, ground cover shrub (*Gaultheria procumbens*), plus polyanthus and* Iris reticulata *for spring interest.*

Above: *For maximum impact, fill the windowbox full of plants. Ivy-leaved and zonal pelargoniums provide the main display, with* Argyranthemum *buds waiting to come out and a pink verbena at bottom left foreground.*

Right: *This symmetrical display features Grevillea for central foliage, ivy-leaved pelargoniums and Helichrysum 'Limelight'.*

Begonia semperflorens *flank the focal point of the Grevillea.*

Above: *These busy lizzies are ideal for a windowbox that does not get much sun. They actually prefer light dappled shade. If the plants are in flower at the time of planting, they will carry on.*

Below: *Pansies make a good, long-lasting display and associate well with ivies. Universal strain pansies are ideal for winter displays. To keep them flowering, deadhead them regularly.*

Planting up a wooden barrel

Wooden half barrels are the favorite choice for permanently planting woodland shrubs, such as dwarf rhododendron, pieris or camellia, as they go so well together. You will need a large barrel, but do not choose one larger than you can comfortably move when it is full of soil. A 12in(30cm) container is the very smallest you should consider; 15-18in(38-45cm) is better and 24in(60cm) the ultimate. The larger the container, the larger the plant will be able to grow, because there will be more room for the roots. In a small pot the plant will be naturally dwarfed, but it will also dry out very quickly and need more frequent watering.

The rhododendron featured here is a lime-hating plant that needs to be planted in a lime-free potting mixture and not the normal kind. Special lime-free (ericaceous) potting mixtures are available, but these do not normally contain soil, being based on peat or coir instead. On their own, they are not ideal for plants that will be left in the same container for several years. You can make up your own mixture, consisting of half ericaceous soil and half soil-based potting material. There is a little lime in this, but the mixture seems to suit ericaceous plants. If you prefer to plant other shrubs, choose reasonably compact kinds and fill the container with normal soil-based potting mix.

1 *Allow the plastic sheet to hang over the sides of the barrel. Partly fill the barrel with a mixture of ericaceous and soil-based potting mix.*

Treating a wooden barrel

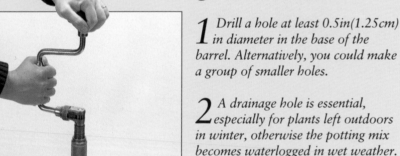

1 *Drill a hole at least 0.5in(1.25cm) in diameter in the base of the barrel. Alternatively, you could make a group of smaller holes.*

2 *A drainage hole is essential, especially for plants left outdoors in winter, otherwise the potting mix becomes waterlogged in wet weather.*

3 *Paint the barrel inside and out (including the base) with plant-friendly wood preservative. To allow any paint fumes to disappear, leave the barrel to dry out completely for a few days before proceeding.*

4 *Take a square of unperforated plastic at least four times as wide as the barrel, lay it over the top and push the middle down to form a loose lining. Push the center 2in(5cm) out through the hole in the base.*

4 Roll back the remaining plastic and tuck it neatly inside the edge of the barrel so that it does not show. In this way, the plastic becomes a 'collar' that prevents the compost touching the wood. Again, this is to prevent the risk of rotting the wood.

2 Knock the plant out of its pot and place it in the center of the barrel. If the pot is filled with roots, gently tease a few of them out first, otherwise they will not be able to grow out into the compost.

3 Cut away some of the surplus plastic, leaving about 2in(5cm) all round the rim of the barrel. Press the sheet roughly against the edges of the barrel to give a reasonable fit. Do not worry about the folds that develop.

5 Cut the tip off the plastic sheet protruding through the hole in the base of the barrel. This allows the excess water to drain away from the potting soil without wetting the wood and thus reduces the risk of rotting.

5 Fill round the roots with more potting mix, leaving the top of the rootball level with the surface. The plant should be no deeper in the barrel than it was in the original pot.

Leave 1in(2.5cm)
between the soil surface
and the rim of the barrel
for watering.

6 Water the plant in well, so that the potting mix is thoroughly moist. Check it at least once a week and water again whenever the soil feels dry when you press a finger in it.

A pot for a shady place

Since most of the plants traditionally grown in containers are sun-lovers, shady areas can be some of the most difficult to 'decorate' with pots. However, many plants that are suitable for shady gardens grow well in containers. Hydrangeas and clumps of hostas make good specimen plants to grow on their own in large pots. Small plants make more of a show when grouped together in large containers. All the plants featured here are moisture lovers, so select a container that retains moisture well and looks at home in moist shady conditions. The one shown here is a fiber pot, made from recycled paper. This type of container will biodegrade after a few years in the garden, but is not expensive to buy. Good plants for growing in containers in shade include lady's mantle (*Alchemilla mollis*), *Ajuga* (ornamental bugle, which has colored leaves and blue flowers), cultivated celandines, *Pulmonaria* (lungwort), which has silver spotted leaves, *Brunnera* (perennial forget-me-not), plus camellia and miniature rhododendrons (see page 26-27). Few annuals will tolerate shade for more than half a day, but *Impatiens* (busy lizzie) will thrive if they are already flowering when you plant them.

4 Plant the foliage plant first - here a hardy fern - and add the flowering plants next. Knock each one carefully out of its pot and plant it without breaking up the ball of roots.

1 Large fiber pots may have several holes around the sides of the base, rather than one large one in the middle, as you find with many containers. Cover each hole with a 'crock' to keep the compost in.

2 Fill the pot to within 2in(5cm) of its rim with soil-based potting mixture. This will suit the perennials to be planted here, as they will remain in the container for several years and its weight keeps the pot stable.

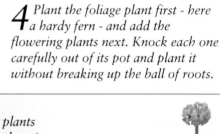

3 Choose the plants and, leaving them in their pots for the time being, stand them together in the container while you decide which ones look best next to each other.

5 Finish off by tucking a few trailing plants, such as the ivies used here, around the sides to soften the edge of the container. Alternative edging plants for shade include Ajuga *(bugle)* and Alchemilla mollis *(lady's mantle)*.

6 Trickle a few handfuls of potting mixture between the plants to fill any gaps and leave the surface level. Check that the plants are left growing at the same depth as they were when planted in their original pots.

7 As a finishing touch, twist the trails of ivy together to form a definite edge to the planting, instead of letting them dangle over the sides. Hold the ends in place with 'twist ties' (paper-covered wire).

Hardy fern
(Dryopteris filix-mas
'Crispula Crispata')

Drumstick primula
(Primula denticulata)

Ivy
(Hedera helix)

Primrose
(Primula
vulgaris)

Viola
labradorica

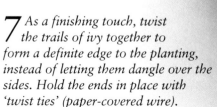

47

Planting up a plastic urn

A formal container such as an urn looks best teamed with a similarly formal style of planting. The traditional scheme shown here uses a tall foliage plant in the middle of the urn, with smaller flowering ones around the edge. It could stand in the middle of a small formal courtyard garden or patio, or on a corner or next to a doorway where it looks good from every angle. The upright conifer in the center adds to the feeling of formality because of its shape. The same plant could be left permanently as a centerpiece, while several changes of annuals are planted around it in successive springs and summers. When it grows too big for the urn or its roots take up all the space so that there is no room to plant anything else, it can be replaced. When this happens, perhaps after two years, you can put the original plant in the garden or feature it as a specimen plant in a big pot. Alternatively, you could make a temporary display by plunging all the plants in their pots up to their rims in the urn and lifting them out as they finish flowering or when you fancy a change of plants.

1 Drill a drainage hole if there is not one already there. Most plastic containers have positions marked where the plastic is thinner to make drilling easier.

2 Cover the drainage hole with a 'crock' - a concave piece of broken flowerpot. This is to stop the potting mix running out through the hole when you water.

4 Loosely fill the container with potting mixture to within 2in(5cm) of the rim. A soilless one will be quite suitable for the conifer and annuals to be planted in this container.

3 Add a trowelful of grit to the bottom of the container to provide extra drainage and prevent the soil being washed out under the crock. Use potting grit, which is a fine grade and ideal for this purpose.

If you are reusing a plastic container, first wash it out thoroughly and remove stuck-on roots. It should be as clean and smooth on the inside as on the outside.

5 Start by planting up the center of the urn. Put the tallest plant here for a symmetrical display. This upright dwarf conifer is ideal.

8 Water the plants well in. As the container is well filled with plants, expect it to dry out quickly. Water it thoroughly every time it feels dry. Do not let the plants dry out and wilt or they will not flower so well.

Chamaecyparis lawsoniana 'Ellwoodii'

Miniature marguerite Chrysanthemum 'Snow Lady'

Bedding tulip

Turk's turban (Ranunculus asiaticus)

Bellis perennis 'Goliath'

Ajuga 'Burgundy Glow'

Bellis perennis 'Pomponette'

6 Plant the edge of the urn with flowering plants, such as the Ranunculus, bellis daisies, miniature marguerite and Ajuga. They contrast well with the foliage in the center.

7 When planting is complete, top up any hollows between the plants with enough potting mixture to fill the container to within 1in(2.5cm) of the rim and leave the surface level.

49

Bulbs for spring displays

Rather than leaving containers empty in winter, after you have pulled out the summer bedding, why not plant bulbs? All you need are durable, weatherproof containers. Wood, stone and good-quality plastics are all suitable for outdoor winter use and frost-proof terracotta and ceramic pots are available, too. Most bulbs can be planted in the early fall, although tulips are late-rooting and best not planted until mid fall. Once planted, just water the containers lightly and protect them from excess rain until the young shoots start to appear. For winter color, plant the bulbs with ivies, euonymus or other small evergreens. Do not keep tubs of bulbs in the greenhouse until they are in flower and then expect them to survive outdoors - the flowers will not be used to wind and rain. Instead, move tubs to their display positions as soon as the first green shoots appear. In this way, the emerging plants will be quite hardened to the conditions by the time the flowers appear. If you forget to buy bulbs in the fall, you can buy the plants growing in pots in garden centers in spring. Often, they coincide with other spring bedding, such as polyanthus, so it is easy to put together an instant display. When planting bulbs from pots, avoid disturbing the ball of roots; this can give them such a check that they do not flower properly or the leaves start to turn yellow. It is often easier to plunge pots of bulbs up to the rim into an existing display.

Right: Narcissi and Anemone blanda in a spring garden, surrounded by ivy. Plant the bulbs out in the garden after flowering and replace the soil in the tub, ready for the summer annuals.

Left: Paperwhite narcissi planted with polyanthus and winter-flowering pansies. These narcissi are less hardy than most and need a particularly mild, sheltered situation outdoors.

Left: *Choose short, delicate daffodils for growing in containers; many of the ones that look good in gardens are too tall for tubs - the stems break easily and the flowers look top heavy.*

Below: *Formal-looking, hybrid tulips look best in formal containers with a symmetrical planting scheme. The feet underneath the pot raise it up just enough to provide better drainage.*

Below: *Bulbs grown in individual pots can be brought indoors when the buds are showing their true color. Stand them in a plastic-lined basket surrounded by moss to hide the pots. Hyacinths - in shades of blue, purple, pink, red, white and yellow - provide a heady scent in early spring.*

51

Planting tulips in a container

Tulips are another good group of bulbs for containers. If your garden does not provide the conditions they need - well-drained soil and a warm sheltered spot - growing in containers is the best way of catering for them. There are lots of different types of tulips. The earliest to flower are waterlily tulips - the kaufmanniana and fosterii hybrids. These are neat compact plants, with sturdy flowers that open out wide like waterlilies in the sun. They flower at early daffodil time. Greigii hybrid tulips look very similar, but have vividly variegated leaves, dappled with red or purplish splotches, that contrast well with the brightly colored flowers. They flower a few weeks later. These are all compact and ideal for containers. Team them with tubs of spring bedding plants, such as wallflowers, polyanthus, violas, forget-me-nots and bellis daisies for a dazzling display.

Most other tulips flower later, in early summer. These can also be grown in containers, but they need a well-sheltered spot, as their taller stems are very fragile. Tulips should be planted after daffodils, in mid-fall, to prevent the bulbs rotting - they start rooting later. Feed and water the growing tulips as you would other bulbs in containers. After the flowers are over, tip the plants out and transplant them temporarily to some spare ground. When the leaves have died down naturally, dig up the bulbs and let them dry off completely. Twist off any dead foliage or stems, and store the dry bulbs in a cool, dry, dark place for the summer. The early-flowering hybrids mentioned above can then be replanted on a rockery in the garden; tall tulips need a well-drained flowerbed. Unlike many spring bulbs, tulips do best if they are dug up and stored dry for the summer as they easily rot if left in the ground.

2 Put 1-2in(2.5-5cm) of coarse gravel in the bottom of the trough. This prevents the drainage holes from clogging with potting mix. There is no need to cover small holes with crocks. Smooth out the gravel to make it level.

3 Add 1-2in(2.5-5cm) of soil- or peat-based potting mix. You can use up any remaining mixture left over from summer.

4 Remove the dead, brown, outer skins from the tulip bulbs. This helps them to root well and removes any lingering disease spores that may be present on the old skin.

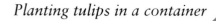

5 We are planting five different varieties in this trough, so we have decided to plant them in five groups of five rather than mixing them up. Press bulbs lightly down into the soil.

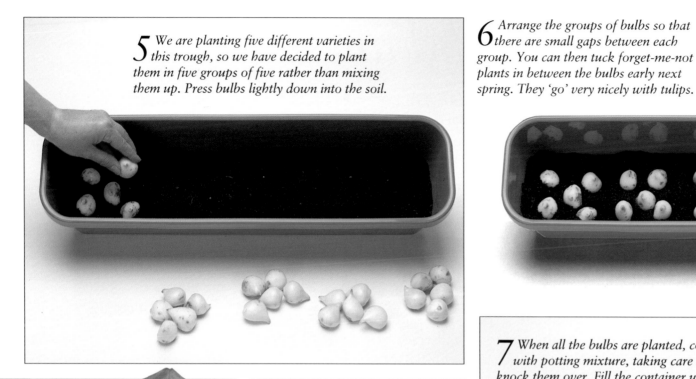

6 Arrange the groups of bulbs so that there are small gaps between each group. You can then tuck forget-me-not plants in between the bulbs early next spring. They 'go' very nicely with tulips.

7 When all the bulbs are planted, cover them with potting mixture, taking care not to knock them over. Fill the container with more soil to within 0.5in(1.25cm) of the rim .

Below: These healthy tulip bulbs have been cleaned of their dead, outer skins and planted in a trough. This planting depth is fine for this container.

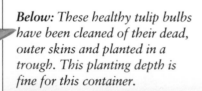

8 Water the soil all over so that it is uniformly moist, but not saturated. Tulips rot easily if kept too damp. Stand the trough in a sheltered spot.

Left: 'Red Riding Hood' is one of the Greigii hybrids (peacock tulips) whose flowers open in the sun to show their centers. The leaves of this variety are mottled with dark purple streaks.

Planting daffodils and anemones

With daffodils, tulips and hyacinths in containers, a patio can be a riot of color from early spring onwards. Dry bulbs are on sale in garden centers in the fall. Buy daffodils as soon as they are available and plant them straightaway, as they start rooting earlier than many spring bulbs. Choose compact bulb varieties, as tall-stemmed kinds may get broken by breezes eddying around a patio. The bulbs should be plump and healthy, without any cuts and bruises or moldy bits; the biggest bulbs will bear the most flowers. You can plant containers entirely with one kind of bulb, but if you want to mix them, choose bulbs that flower at roughly the same time. When it comes to planting, there is no need to use bulb fiber, which is intended for indoor use. Normal peat- or soil-based potting mixture is fine. After planting, stand the containers outdoors in a cool, shady spot protected from heavy rain. (Very often they will be fine in a shady part of the patio next to a wall, since the wall deflects most of the rain). When the first shoots appear, move the containers to their positions on the patio. While the bulbs are flowering, feed them weekly with general-purpose liquid feed. When they are over, tip them out and plant them in the garden. You can then reuse the container for a summer bedding scheme. Buy new bulbs for the following year's container display, as they will flower better than the old ones.

4 Press each bulb gently down into the potting mixture, giving it a half turn. This ensures that the base of the bulb makes good contact with the soil - essential for rooting.

1 If your container does not have drainage holes in the base, you should drill some. It is vital that containers that will be standing outdoors during the winter can drain freely.

2 Place 1-2in(2.5-5cm) of coarse gravel over the base of the container to aid drainage. Bulbs can easily rot if the potting mix is too wet.

3 Put 1-2in(2.5-5cm) of potting mixture over the gravel. Ideally, bulbs should be planted with twice their own depth of potting mix above the tip of the bulb, but this may not be possible in containers.

5 *The more bulbs you get in, the better the display will be. Put the bulbs as close together as you can, without allowing them to touch each other or the sides of the container.*

6 *Cover the bulbs with just enough potting mix to leave the tips on show so you can see where they are when you plant the second layer above.*

7 *Gently press in some more bulbs between the tips of the lower layer. A few Anemone blanda corms will make a contrast with the daffodils.*

Below: *This cross section shows the layers of bulbs in the container, with the daffodils 'Golden Harvest' below and the Anemone blanda 'Blue Shade' dotted above them.*

Right: Anemone blanda *grows to 6in(15cm) and is usually available in mixed colors, although separate shades are sometimes sold. Blue is one of the most popular.*

8 *For a good display, dot another layer of Anemone blanda evenly over the surface, about 1in(2.5cm)above the last. Then fill the container to the rim with potting mix.*

Right: *The daffodil 'Golden Harvest' is a traditional variety once used for cut flower production but now a garden favorite. The daffodils will do best if the container is placed in the sun, but they tolerate light shade.*

9 *Cover this layer of bulbs with a little more soil, leaving it roughly level on top. Take care not to knock over the bulbs, as they are still quite unstable.*

55

Spring annuals - pansies

If you grow your own spring annuals, such as wallflowers, stocks and bellis daisies from seed, you could plant containers in late summer or early autumn, after the summer bedding plants have come out, for a display the following spring. But they need careful attention in winter, and it is much less trouble to leave the plants in trays or small pots in a cold greenhouse and plant them just as they are coming into flower in spring. If you prefer to buy in your plants, you will find plenty of spring annuals to choose from. Forget-me-nots, spring bulbs growing in individual pots, and pansies are some of the most popular. The temptation is often to plant up the greatest mixture of flowers that will fit into a large container, but as a change, try teaming a prettily patterned pot with flowers that pick out one of the colors from the pot. The result will look lovely on an outdoor window ledge or standing in the middle of a patio table. Or try standing a row of similar pots in a row along the top of a low wall. Pansies are particularly attractive and are available in a good range of colors, some with delightful 'faces'.

2 Pack as many plants as possible into the pot for a good display. A small pot like this takes four. Loosely fill the pot with potting mixture to within 1in(2.5cm) of the rim.

1 Start in the usual way by covering the drainage hole in the bottom of the pot with a small crock.

3 *Carefully push each plant out of its pot through the hole in the base. You may need to squeeze the rootballs gently in order to fit them into the container.*

Four plants are enough to fill a small pot. This one measures 20cm(8in) in diameter.

Choose plants with plenty of flower and buds for an instant effect. Remove any dead blooms.

5 *If any potting mix has been spilt onto the container during planting, wipe it off so that the pot is clean. Stand the pot on its matching saucer.*

Like most bedding plants, you can keep pansies flowering for a long time simply by removing the dead flowerheads regularly. Another tip for good flowering is to feed the plants regularly with a high potash liquid or soluble feed.

This frost-resistant, ceramic pot is decorated with an oriental-style floral design in purple to echo the pansies.

4 *When they are all in place, fill the gaps between them with potting mixture, leaving about 0.5in(1.25cm) between the top of the soil and the rim of the pot for watering.*

6 *Water the pansies in. As the pot is packed full of plants, it will dry out quite quickly, so check it regularly and especially during hot weather to see if it needs watering again.*

1 *This container is to be planted with a selection of annual flowers, so choose a soilless potting mixture and fill it to just below the rim.*

A *plastic tub of annuals*

Plastic containers are a bit different to work with than some materials. Plastic is not porous, so the compost in it does not dry out so quickly. This is a benefit on hot summer days, but can be a problem at the start of the season, as small, young plants do not use a great deal of water, especially when the weather is cool. It is easy to overwater them, especially if you use a peat-based potting mixture, which holds much more water than other types. Water with care for the first four to five weeks. Another difference lies in the drainage holes. Plastic pots usually have several holes spread around the base. Because the holes are quite small, there is no need to cover them with crocks, especially if you use a soilless potting mixture, which is more fibrous in texture and less likely to trickle out. Some plastic containers are dual purpose so they do not have drainage holes ready made. You can use the pot without holes, for example, when the container is to stand on a floor that you do not want to be marked by water. If you do want holes in the base, knock through the weak points marked, with the tip of a screwdriver. Some people prefer plastic containers for plants that only last one season - typically spring or summer annuals. This is probably a throwback to the days when plastic containers were rather poor quality and often became brittle after a year or two out in the sunlight. A hard frost in winter was often enough to make them disintegrate entirely. But nowadays, good-quality plastics are available that last very much better and can be used outside all year round.

2 *Group a selection of plants to see how they look together. This is a bright color scheme of red, yellow and orange. As one of them is a climber, place a cane in the middle of the tub to support it.*

3 *Plant the center-piece first - here a climbing black-eyed Susan. Tie it loosely to the cane and tie in new stems regularly.*

5 A foliage plant makes a good 'foil' for groups of flowers. This coleus goes very well with the color scheme of the container.

6 The cream and green variegated ornamental cabbage will eventually make a huge rosette shape at the base of the container. By then, the other flowers will have grown quite tall.

7 Water the finished container well. It should look well filled with plants; as they grow, the effect will become even more abundant-looking. Once the container is filled with roots, water it once or twice a day.

4 Arrange the other plants in groups of the same type, next to neighbors that make a strong contrast, with flowers of different sizes, colors and shapes.

Black-eyed Susan (Thunbergia alata)

Argyranthemum frutescens 'Jamaica Primrose'

African marigold, compact type

Ornamental cabbage

Salvia 'Vanguard'

Coleus

French marigold 'Aurora Fire'

59

Variation on a summer theme

Here is an alternative idea for an arrangement of summer flowers in a large plastic pot, using a mixture of flowering annuals, half-hardy perennials and foliage plants in a range of shapes and sizes. The half-hardy perennial is *Anisodontea capensis,* which can be treated rather like a pelargonium. Whatever plants you choose, it is a good idea to stick to a basic formula: a large centerpiece - perhaps a climber on a cane, a standard fuchsia or simply a tall, upright plant; various smaller 'filler' flowers for plenty of color; complementary foliage and either trailing plants or something with large leaves or dangling rosette shapes that will come over the edges of the container. You can make a traditional arrangement in a wide mixture of colors or a more sophisticated one, using part of the spectrum, as here.

As the plants in the display grow up, remember to remove dead flowerheads regularly to encourage plants to keep flowering. Nip out any shoots that grow out of shape or are very overcrowded. Climbers will certainly need regular attention to stop them getting out of control and smothering their neighbors. They normally grow quickly, so go over them every week or two, tying in the new growth. When it reaches the top of the cane, allow it to bend over and then start winding it back down the pillar of foliage. Tie it into place. This way, new flowering shoots will gradually cover the older parts of the stems that are no longer producing new buds.

5 When the roots are planted, untie the plant from the short stick and retie it to the taller cane in the new pot. Use loose ties to avoid bruising.

1 As this pot is to be used outside, drainage holes are essential. Tap out the weak points with a screwdriver and a hammer.

2 The drainage holes are small, so there is no need to cover them with crocks. The potting mixture is fibrous peat that is unlikely to trickle out. Fill the container to just below the rim.

3 The centerpiece is a tall climbing plant, so push a cane firmly down through the soil in the middle of the pot until it reaches the base. If you prefer, make a tripod of canes.

4 Plant the climber alongside the cane. Leave it tied to its existing stick while you plant it, otherwise you will have trailing stems around you that could easily get broken.

6 Arrange the remaining plants around the container. Put contrasting shapes and sizes next to each other, especially if the display has a color theme.

7 Knock the plants out of their pots and tuck them into place. For a good display, fill the container well, compressing the rootballs slightly to fit the spaces.

Purple bell vine, (Rhodochiton atrosanguineus)

Anisodontea capensis, a shrubby half-hardy perennial.

8 Use small plants at the base of larger ones to hide bare stems or too many leaves. Drape a few large leaves over the edge of the tub to soften its appearance. Fill every gap!

Impatiens 'Accent Lilac'

Viola 'Prince Henry'

Mauve and purple variegated ornamental cabbage

9 Water the container well and often. As the roots fill the space, expect the display to need even more watering and feeding to keep it looking its best.

61

A taste of the Orient

Exotic plants and containers are easy to obtain and by teaming them together you can create some very interesting effects. Oriental pots are specially attractive. They are frost-resistant and available in a wide range of sizes and designs, often with matching saucers. To continue the oriental theme, you could plant them with a trimmed conifer, flowering quince (*Chaenomeles*) or Japanese maple (*Acer*) - one per pot - to give a suggestion of bonsai trees. Another good choice would be bamboo. Despite the huge size to which some species grow, bamboos make first-class container plants. Choose any of the normal varieties found in garden centers, such as the *Arundinaria japonica* shown here. All the above plants are woody perennials and if they are to remain in the container permanently, use a soil-based planting mix. Choose a pot and plant that are in proportion to each other. A large plant and pot can look good on their own or try a collection of three or five smaller ones of different sizes to make a group. For an oriental-looking background, stand the pot on a patch of raked gravel or on a raised platform with trelliswork behind it. All the suggested plants grow relatively slowly and can be planted in the garden or repotted when they outgrow their tubs.

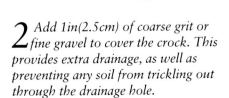

1 Start by putting a 'crock' - a piece of broken clay flowerpot - over the drainage hole in the base of the pot to stop the potting mix running out when you water the container.

2 Add 1in(2.5cm) of coarse grit or fine gravel to cover the crock. This provides extra drainage, as well as preventing any soil from trickling out through the drainage hole.

3 Put a handful or two of potting mixture in the pot, so that the roots of the bamboo do not stand directly on the grit when it is planted.

4 Knock the plant out of its pot. Tap the side of the pot firmly onto a hard surface to loosen the plant.

This container was chosen because it has a bamboo design to match the planting.

5 Sit the plant in position in the middle of its pot. Check that the top of the rootball comes to about 1in(2.5cm) below the rim of the pot. If not, lift it out and either add or remove soil to bring it to the correct level.

Use a soil-based potting mixture, as it is heavier than the soilless types and will help to keep the pot stable. It also 'lasts' longer, so is better for permanent pot planting.

6 Fill the gap between the rootball and the sides of the container with more of the same potting mixture and firm it in very lightly to make sure that the pot is completely filled.

7 Move the plant to the required position, sit it on its matching saucer and water the plant in well. If the soil level sinks slightly, top up the pot and water it lightly once more to settle it.

We tend to think of bamboos as plants that like very wet conditions, but in fact they prefer reasonable drainage, which is readily provided in containers. They will tolerate some drought, but try to keep them well watered while they are actively growing during the summer.

Below: Green plants in different sizes of matching pots make a restful group for a seating area. Tall plants, such as the bay tree shown here, make a discreet and portable screen.

Planted pots galore

A patio certainly would not look right without potted plants, but containers can be used in many more ways, all around the garden. You can use a group of them, in different sizes, to decorate a large expanse of hard surfacing, such as a path or driveway. Stand them next to doors or gates for emphasis, or next to seats to provide close detail by way of contrast with a more distant view. Seats and entrances are an ideal place to put containers of scented plants. Containers can also solve certain gardening problems. For example, if your border develops an odd gap later in the season, you can stand a container of flowering plants on the spot. If the ground is soft, lay a small paving slab on the soil to provide a firm base for the pot. A low-growing garden, such as one specially for herbs, can be given some welcome height by using tall containers - old chimney pots, for example - planted with 'herby' flowers, including nasturtium. Containers are a good way of introducing instant color to an area that is in need of a quick 'lift'. And use them to camouflage manhole covers. A container big enough to sit over the top is perfect; choose a slightly squat one, so that when filled with plants and potting mix it is not too heavy to move if you need to get at the plumbing below.

Right: Entrances are a good setting for containers. The size of the container and the entrance should be in scale with each other. Here, the gate seems to 'frame' the container and its plants.

Deadhead the flowers
regularly to keep the
display looking fresh.

Above: Containers can add height,
detail or color to a border. Here, the
bright colors of a mosaic pot and the
French lavender in it echo the colors
found elsewhere in this busy border.

Left: A tall terracotta pot lifts its cargo
of tulips well above the level of the
surrounding spring border, making
them stand out. Terracotta pots
contrast well with areas of foliage.

Right: Use colorful containers in a
conservatory or sunroom for a splash
of seasonal color. Choose tough
plants, such as pelargoniums, that are
not very prone to pest problems.

65

Planting a large traditional hanging basket

Traditional hanging baskets are made of an open latticework of wire. This makes it possible to plant not only the top, but the sides and base of the basket as well, to create a perfect ball of bloom. Wire baskets must be lined before they can hold any potting mix. Although you could use any of the basket liners available in garden centers, or even black plastic, live moss is the traditional choice and certainly looks best. Sphagnum moss is sold ready-bagged in garden centers for this purpose. If possible, take a look at it first and choose fresh, green, live moss, which makes an attractive background for basket plants. Moss that has been allowed to dry out and turn brown will not green up again later. Some people recommend raking moss out of the lawn to use in hanging baskets. Although it looks green to start with, moss obtained this way quickly goes brown after the basket has been planted. If you are planting a traditional hanging basket, it is a good idea to stick to a traditional type of planting scheme. This basically involves using a mixture of plants - trailers, upright and even sometimes small climbers - in a wide range of colors. Traditional favorites include the plants shown in this attractive arrangement - ivy-leaved pelargoniums (the trailing kind, often referred to as geraniums), petunias, trailing lobelias, and both trailing and upright fuchsias. Other annual bedding plants are often used, too - French marigolds and busy lizzie, for instance - while tuberous begonias, available as both upright and trailing varieties, are also good choices.

5 Lay a second tier of trailing plants (in this case more lobelia), so that they rest between the first row of plants and a few inches above them.

1 Traditional wire baskets have a rounded base, so sit them in a bucket to hold them firmly while you plant them up. Line the bottom with tight wads of moss for a firm base.

2 Trailing lobelia is suitable for the sides and base of the basket. Press the plants carefully out of their trays with a finger or the tip of a pencil or cane to avoid damaging the roots.

3 Lay the plants on their sides, with their roots on the mossy base and the stems hanging out from the lower edge of the basket. Add a little soil to hold the roots in place if you wish.

4 Add another layer of moss to the edge of the basket until about half the sides are covered. Dense wads of moss will retain the soil more effectively than loose fluffy strands.

Ivy leaved geranium
'Amethyst'

Upright fuchsia
'Beacon Rosa'

Purple petunia

Petunia 'Pink vein'

Verbena
'Carousel'

6 *Continue adding moss right up to the rim or slightly above it. Add soilless potting mixture to the center of the basket, filling the gaps around the rootballs of the plants that have already been put in.*

Lobelia
'Fountain'

Trailing fuchsia
'Frank Saunders'

7 *Plant the top of the basket with a mixture of upright and trailing plants. Knock them out of their pots first and plant them closely together so the basket looks full from the start.*

8 *Lift the chains carefully to avoid damaging the plants. Hang the basket in a sheltered sunny place. Water it well in, and water daily to prevent the soil drying out.*

Using a rigid liner

Superb though they undoubtedly look, traditional wire hanging baskets suffer from one major drawback. If you line them with moss, they dry out quickly and are very difficult to rewet. If you do not favor a plastic, solid-sided hanging basket, one solution is to try a different liner. Fiber liners, made of recycled paper, resemble compressed peat, but the liner is far less porous than moss. The fiber sides soak up water, which helps to keep the compost moist. Unless the basket is heavily overwatered, it won't drip as much as moss-lined baskets tend to do. The one disadvantage of preformed fiber liners is that you cannot plant through the sides and base. If you cut holes in the liner, you run the risk of compost washing out, as well as water dripping, so it is better not to do so. Even so, by planting plenty of trailing plants at both the sides and top of the basket, you can still achieve a very pretty, traditional-looking basket, without the hard work associated with moss. To achieve a 'ball of bloom look', space out the stems of trailing plants around the basket and tie them down onto the wire frame. This stops the ends of the shoots turning up towards the light and encourages them to branch out, which gives the basket a better covering. As with any hanging basket, check the potting mix at least once a day and water it well as soon as it begins to feel dry - or even slightly before. If you did not add a slow-release fertilizer when the basket was planted, be sure to feed it regularly - at least once a week - with a good liquid or soluble feed to keep the plants flowering well. Nip off the dead flowerheads for the same reason.

3 Stand the basket on top of a bucket to hold it upright. The ivy-leaved pelargonium in the center stays reasonably upright if surrounded by other plants.

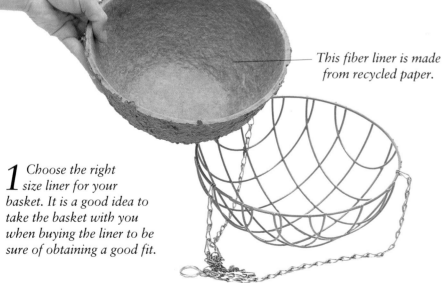

This fiber liner is made from recycled paper.

1 Choose the right size liner for your basket. It is a good idea to take the basket with you when buying the liner to be sure of obtaining a good fit.

2 Place the liner in the basket and fill it with potting mixture. Choose suitable plants and knock them out of their pots before planting them in the liner.

Soilless mixes are ideal for hanging baskets.

Ivy-leaved
geranium 'Beauty
of Eastbourne'

Lobelia 'Sapphire'

4 *Finish off by tucking small trailing lobelias into the gaps between the larger plants. These will cascade over the sides, hiding most of the liner from view.*

Miniature regal
pelargonium

Pink petunia

5 *Lift the chains carefully over the plants and hang up the finished basket in its final position. Water it in thoroughly. The basket will need this good soaking to start with, as the fiber liner absorbs a great deal of water.*

69

Using a flexible basket liner

1 *Place a flexible liner inside the basket. Press it well down and overlap adjacent panels to achieve a good fit.*

Many types of natural and synthetic flexible liners are available for use with traditional wire hanging baskets. These offer the best possible compromise between moss and a rigid liner. Flexible liners are made from a series of panels that, when pushed down inside the basket, overlap slightly to take up the shape of the container. They can be made of foam plastic, coconut fiber or the rather less flexible 'whalehide'. The advantage of this type of liner is that, where the panels overlap, you are left with small slits through which you can put the plants. This makes it possible to create the spectacular 'ball of bloom', characteristic of a traditional moss-lined basket. However, because the liner is made of a more water-retentive material, the basket will not dry out or drip as much as a mossed one. As with a traditional moss-lined basket, it is good idea to place an old saucer or circle of plastic into the base of the basket after lining, which helps to stop the water dripping straight out through the bottom. When planting a traditional wire basket - which has a rounded base - stand it inside the top of a bucket for support. Start with the difficult areas - the sides - by planting as low down as you can, as this will give a better result. Then plant the top. Aim to pack as many plants into the basket as you can for maximum impact. If you think that the basket may be difficult to water once it is full, try a useful tip. Cut a few inches from the neck end of a plastic bottle and make a funnel (see page 19). Sink this into the middle of the basket, hidden between the plants, with just the top above soil level. Then, every time you water, fill the funnel and water will trickle down into the heart of the basket instead of running away down the sides.

2 *Plant the sides by pushing the plant roots through the slits between the panels. Then tuck the edges of the panels firmly around the plants to prevent soil from leaking out.*

3 *Fill the basket to the rim with potting mixture, making sure it completely surrounds the roots of the plants that have already been put in.*

4 *Next, begin planting the top of the basket. These three bushy fuchsias will give some height among the other plants, which are predominantly trailing species.*

5 *Plant an ivy-leaved pelargonium and petunias in the gaps between the fuchsias. Knock all the plants out of their pots first.*

6 *Firm each plant gently in, leaving a shallow depression around the inside edge of the basket to make watering easier. If the basket is overfilled, water bounces off the top.*

Single red petunia

Ivy-leaved pelargonium 'Scarlet Galilee'

Fuchsia 'Meike Meursing'

Helichrysum microphylla

Pink and red impatiens

7 *As a finishing touch, spread out the long shoots of fuchsia and other plants evenly around the sides of the basket and fix them to the wire framework using flexible plant ties.*

8 *Finally, gather up the chains, taking care not to damage the plants, and hang up the basket. Water it well, allowing the potting mixture to absorb some of the water before adding more, until it is moist through.*

Rescuing a dried-out hanging basket

Containers do not take a great deal of time to look after, but they need attention little and often to keep them looking their best. The important thing to remember is that containers need more water as the plants in them grow bigger. Large plants use more water and feed than when they were small, and once their roots fill the soil, there is less room for water. If you miss the odd watering, feeding and deadheading, it is amazing how quickly the display suffers. But do not feel too bad about it - it happens to all of us once in a while, especially when we are busy or away from home a lot. As long as the plants are not completely dead, the container can usually be revived. The first problem is to get some water into the soil. Unless you used water-retaining gel crystals in the soil before planting, you will find that dried out potting mix is very difficult to rewet. In fact, it is virtually waterproof. If you pour water into the top of the container, it just runs out around the sides without wetting the center. To combat this, try adding a tiny drop of liquid detergent to the water as a wetting agent. The simplest solution is to stand the container in a deep bowl of water for a couple of hours and let it have a really good soak until the soil is saturated. Here we show how to rescue and tidy up a typical 'lost cause.'

1 *This moss-lined basket has been rather neglected; not only is the soil bone dry and the moss yellow, but the flowers need deadheading, trimming and tying up into place.*

2 *Start by snipping off the dead flowerheads - this makes the basket look better straightaway. Remove any dead, damaged or browning leaves at the same time.*

3 *Where there are no buds on the same shoot to follow on, such as on this dianthus, cut complete stems back close to the base to encourage a new crop of shoots and buds.*

4 *Plants with trailing stems often become tangled and droop down around the basket instead of growing up over it. Tease them apart and see which pieces are worth keeping.*

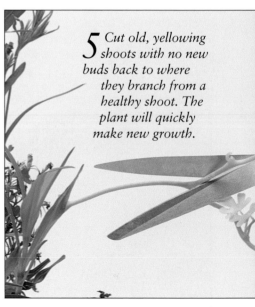

5 *Cut old, yellowing shoots with no new buds back to where they branch from a healthy shoot. The plant will quickly make new growth.*

7 As you tidy the basket, you will remove a lot of material. The basket will look better for it, however, and it is quicker than trying to revive dead pieces.

Canary creeper (Tropaeolum peregrinum) looks neater tied to the chain.

Trailing lobelia is easy to keep tidy.

Tuberous begonias respond well to deadheading.

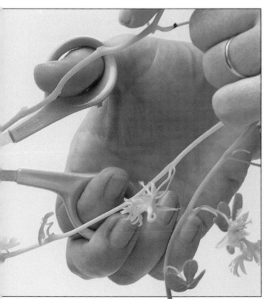

8 Stand the basket in a deep bowl of tepid water for at least an hour and spray more water over the plants to give them a quick pick-me-up. This also makes it easier for bone-dry potting mix to start absorbing water.

Use a cane to support the chains while the basket is soaking.

A small hand sprayer is ideal for misting the plants.

6 Tie back healthy green shoots with plenty of flower, using loose twist ties or thin string. Trailing and climbing plants look best growing up the chains or trained round the sides.

9 Top up the basket with a watering can until it is fully saturated. Do not feed dry plants - wait a few days.

Regenerating a lopsided hanging basket

In a perfect garden, plants in containers and hanging baskets would grow evenly, making a symmetrical shape. They would fill the container and spill attractively over the edges all round. But in practice, things do not always go quite according to plan. Container plants sometimes grow lopsided. This is most likely to happen if they are close to a wall, where they receive light from one side while the other is in heavy shade - in the same way as houseplants growing on a windowsill indoors lean towards the light. The remedy in both cases is the same. Turn the containers round every week or two, so that both sides have a turn in the light. But this is not always the problem. Because of their shape, some plants naturally grow to one side more than the other. This is why it is a good idea to choose well-shaped bushy specimens in the first place. (If you raise plants from seed or cuttings, nip the growing tips out when they are 2-3in(5-7.5cm) high.) You can also help prevent plants growing lopsided by checking them over each time you water or deadhead them, and nipping out any shoots that are growing out of place. You can cut straggly or one-sided growth back quite hard. This encourages the plant to branch out from lower down, producing several shoots where there was previously one.

1 This hanging basket has been growing close to a wall, where one side was in deep shade. Because it has not been turned round regularly, the plants have all grown over to one side.

2 With the basket still hanging up, have a quick tidy up and snip off all the dead flowerheads. With fuchsias, take off the heads where the flower stems join the main plant stem.

3 At the same time, remove any dead, yellow or disfigured leaves, as they spoil the look of the display. Remove old pelargonium leaves, as here, at the base of the leaf stalk.

4 Lift the basket down carefully from its bracket. To avoid damaging any plants that are trailing down round the sides, stand it in the top of a bucket while you work on it.

If you need more height, stand the bucket on an upturned bowl.

5 *Continue removing any dead leaves and flowers as you find them. Spread out the stems gently so as to avoid snapping them, and space them out all round the basket. Tie them in position around the rim with plant ties.*

These green twist ties are excellent for tying in stems

Fuchsia 'Dancing Flame'

Pelargonium 'Mexicana'

6 *Separate long trailing stems that have become tangled together and spread them out as much as possible all round the basket to give it a more even coverage.*

8 *The finished result may not be entirely perfect but it is certainly very much better than it was. To maintain the improvement, tie new stems in regularly to keep the display in shape.*

7 *When the basket is hanging back up on its bracket, tie these stems in place evenly over the underside of the basket - this creates a much more impressive-looking sphere of flowers.*

1 *Fill the container with potting mixture to within 2in(5cm) of the rim; this allows room for the rootballs of the plants. Choose a soil-free mixture, as it is lightweight.*

2 *Group the plants around the container to create an interesting scheme. Choose foliage plants with trailing stems and a variety of leaf shapes and colors for contrast.*

Indoor hanging baskets

Hanging baskets are not only decorative outdoors; you can also use them to create unusual arrangements in a sunroom, conservatory or even an ornamental greenhouse. This is a good way to display trailing indoor plants, such as asparagus fern, that sprawl untidily when grown in normal pots and are difficult to accommodate. You can make up mixed displays, as shown here, or use a basket to grow a single specimen plant. Both trailing and climbing plants can be grown successfully in this way. (With climbers, twine the stems around the basket and let them grow up the chains, as well as dangling over the edges.) Wax plants (*Hoya*), stephanotis and columneas all make good specimen plants. Indoor baskets are also a good way of growing some outdoor plants that have large, fragile flowers, such as morning glory, black-eyed Susan, and the large, frilly, double petunias, all of which are easily spoiled by bad weather outside. If the conservatory is in a very sunny spot, it is a good idea to fix blinds or apply shading paint to the windows in summer to prevent the plants from scorching. Plants are particularly at risk when growing close to the glass, as is the case with hanging baskets. Shading not only cuts down direct light, but also helps to stop the room becoming too hot, which can also be harmful to plants. Try to prevent the temperature rising above 86°F(30°C) by providing plenty of ventilation and, if possible, using an electric fan to circulate cool air around the plants.

When it comes to choosing containers for indoors, you can use the same types of basket as you would have in the garden. However, unless they are supplied with drip trays, they are likely to make a mess of the floor, as they tend to drip when they are watered. Most people prefer to use the more decorative hanging containers sold especially for conservatories.

3 *Make a pot-sized hole in the center of the basket to take the flowering plant that will form the centrepiece of the arrangement.*

Piggyback plant (Tolmiea menziesii)

Kalanchoe blossfeldiana

4 *Since the flowers of this plant will only last a few weeks, 'plunge' it, still in its pot, into the basket. Later on, you can easily replace it without disturbing the other plants.*

Asparagus fern (Asparagus sprengeri)

5 *Hang the basket up carefully and water it thoroughly. This container includes an integral drip tray, which avoids water splashing onto the floor and acts as a small water reservoir.*

Ficus pumila 'Variegata'

6 *These plants will enjoy good light, but not strong direct sun. Start feeding with a general-purpose liquid houseplant feed after about four weeks and do not let the soil dry out.*

Spider plant (Chlorophytum comosum vittatum)

Hanging baskets on show

The most effective way to grow trailing plants is in hanging baskets. But now that they have become so popular it is not just traditional summer flowers like fuchsias, pelargoniums and lobelia that are grown in them; hardy annuals such as nasturtiums (which you can put outdoors several weeks before half-hardy bedding plants), herbs, strawberries and even dwarf varieties of tomatoes and other edibles are grown in hanging baskets, too. And as an alternative to trailing plants, some people like to plant a complete basket - sides as well as top - with one kind of compact annual such as busy lizzie, to make a tight-knit sphere of flower. This looks best using mixed colours. Another recent innovation is to plant a normal mixed basket but with very long trailing plants such as *Plectranthus* growing down from the sides to create what almost looks like a beard underneath. Hanging baskets need not only be for summer decoration. In winter, you could replant them with winter-flowering pansies or ivies. For early spring, polyanthus and other spring bedding plants normally used in containers can be put in hanging baskets. A sheltered spot, such as inside a large porch or under a carport, is best for winter and early spring hanging baskets. In the open, they would get buffetting more by the wind than containers at ground level; heavy rain and frost can also spoil them.

Below: A stunning 'ball of bloom', created by planting top, sides and base of a wire-framed basket with ivy-leaved pelargoniums and lobelia. The nearby spider plant adds contrast.

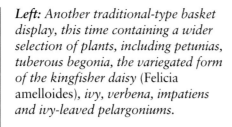

Left: *Another traditional-type basket display, this time containing a wider selection of plants, including petunias, tuberous begonia, the variegated form of the kingfisher daisy (*Felicia amelloides), *ivy, verbena, impatiens and ivy-leaved pelargoniums.*

Right: *Here a single variety of ivy-leaved pelargonium has been used to create a flowering sphere; the effect is very striking, particularly against the white sunlit wall. Single-color baskets can provide a visual 'breather' when teamed with multicolored displays.*

Below: *Matching hanging baskets can be just as eye-catching; here displays of* nasturtiums, lobelia, Calceolaria rugosa - *with the small yellow pouches - and* Senecio bicolor (Cineraria maritima) - *with silver foliage - appear in both baskets.*

A herb hanging basket

As a change from the usual flowering annuals, why not plan a hanging basket of herbs? Herbs are good plants for growing this way, as they are naturally fairly drought-tolerant. A hanging basket is a useful way to grow culinary varieties of herb, as you can put it right outside the kitchen door and it acts as a herbal air freshener, giving the house a pleasant, healthy perfume each time you open the door and brush past the plants. The scent of herbs is also said to deter flies. The best herbs to choose are the popular culinary varieties that are naturally compact, such as bush basil. As the basket will be replanted every spring, you have the chance to replace annual herbs, such as basil and chervil, and also to divide up over-large clumps of perennials, such as mint and chives, so you can replace overgrown plants with small pieces. Rosemary roots easily from cuttings and parsley is a biennial that runs to seed in its second year and needs to be replaced each spring with new seedlings. As well as the taller plants for the center of the basket, you will need a few trailing ones, such as thyme and marjoram, to plant around the sides, just as you would use trailing lobelia in a flowering basket. Choose herbs that offer a wide range of shapes and sizes, including as many as possible with colored leaves or bright flowers. Pick the herbs regularly to keep them neat and bushy, but feed and water them well, so that they can replace 'cropped' growth.

2 *If the plant has a large rootball, plant it from the inside, pushing the top of the plant through the side hole.*

3 *When the side pockets are planted, fill the basket almost to the rim with potting mixture. Tuck it around the roots of the plants in pockets.*

1 *Remove the detachable 'pockets' and plant into them from the inside or the outside, whichever is easier.*

Clip the pocket back once the plant is in place.

4 *Plant the larger herbs in the top of the basket. Some mints can 'take over', but this pineapple mint is a less vigorous variety.*

5 Liven up a herb collection with a few flowers. These tiny violas are a close relative of heartsease, a medicinal herb, but do not try to eat them.

6 When the basket is complete, water it well. Herbs tolerate drier conditions than most bedding plants, but it pays to look after them well so that they remain productive.

7 This container has an integral drip tray that prevents dripping when you water it and also acts as a useful small water reservoir for the plants.

8 Gather up the chains, taking care not to snag or damage the plants. Hang the basket in a sunny but sheltered position, ideally close to the kitchen door for convenience.

A herb hanging basket

Rosemary
(Rosmarinus officinalis)

Garlic chives
(Allium tuberosum)

Pineapple mint

Viola
'Prince Henry'

Curled parsley
(Petroselinum crispum)

Dwarf marjoram
(Origanum vulgare 'Compactum')

Caraway thyme
(Thymus herba-barona)

Planting up a plastic wall planter

1 *If possible, stand the planter on its base while you are planting it. Some do not have a flat base and most are top heavy, so if this is difficult, hang it in its final position and fill it almost to the rim with potting mixture.*

Imagine a hanging basket sliced in half vertically through the middle, with the flat side stuck against a wall. That is a wall planter. Some wall planters are constructed very much like half hanging baskets, with a wire framework that needs lining in much the same way as a traditional hanging basket. If you choose this type, you will also need a liner for it. Special liners are made in a range of sizes to fit. However, unless you have plenty of time for watering, open-sided wall planters can be rather disappointing, as the plants in them dry out almost in front of your eyes. Wall planters with solid sides are generally more practical. Even so, they dry out quite quickly compared to containers at ground level. This is partly because the containers themselves are so much smaller and also because, being raised up, they are surrounded by breezes that cause water to evaporate from the soil faster than usual. Once you have taken these factors into account, wall planters can look most attractive. Being small, they are usually placed in a 'key' position where they are very visible, so be sure to use only the very best plants in them. Formal arrangements are probably the most suitable, but you could experiment with informal ones. These usually work best if you group a collection of planters in the same style at different levels on a wall. You will only need a very few plants, as the wall planter is only half the depth of normal containers.

2 *Formal plantings suit these containers well. Here, the centerpiece is a rather striking coleus. You may need to look through a batch of plants before finding a well-shaped specimen.*

3 *The back row is made up of bedding salvias. From a box of 15 plants, four of the same shape and size were chosen to maintain the symmetrical shape of the design.*

4 *The front row consists of four French marigolds placed in pairs on either side of the coleus. Choose the best plants and use up the rest in other containers or around the garden.*

5 *Avoid breaking up the rootballs when you plant them. If space is restricted, you may need to squeeze the roots slightly to make them fit in. This is no problem if you are careful.*

6 *Fill in the spaces between the rootballs with more soil and scatter some over the surface of the finished display. Unfurl any leaves that have been tucked in.*

Salvia 'Vanguard'

Coleus hybrid

French marigold 'Aurora Fire'

8 *The finished arrangement is likely to dry out more quickly than a container at ground level, so check it twice daily and water it as often as necessary to keep the soil moist.*

7 *As the container is relatively small but well filled, water it two or three times, allowing the water to soak in well before adding any more.*

A chic terracotta wall display

Plain, neutral-colored, classic-style containers are probably the best value plant holders. You can bring them out year after year, planted up with a different set of plants to create a completely new look each time. This terracotta wall planter, for instance, can be planted in several ways. You could choose a traditional plant arrangement, using bedding plants such as tuberous begonias and lobelia as here, or a mediterranean design based on pelargoniums - the trailing ivy-leaved sort are specially suitable for a wall planter like this. You could use herbs for a scented mixture or try a fairly new half-hardy trailing perennial called *Scaveola aemula*; a single plant is enough to fill a container of this size on its own. (It has flowers like mauve-blue fans with yellow centers). Experiment with daring color schemes and bold plant shapes. You can never really tell how plants will look until you see them together, so buy enough for several containers and try out all the possible combinations before deciding which to plant together. You can easily come up with something quite sensational.

For striking results in a container like this - which is really only half a container - it is vital to pack it full of plants. This means, of course, that it will dry out very quickly, so check it regularly and water it as often as necessary to prevent the soil from drying out. Deadhead old blooms regularly and feed at least once a week. In this way, the display will continue to look good throughout the season and right up to the first frosts.

1 This container has a rounded base and will not stand upright, so fill and plant it after it has been fixed to the wall. Fill it almost to the brim with soilless potting mixture.

2 The centerpiece of this display is a lovely rose-pink flowered tuberous begonia. Plant this first, in the middle of the container, taking care not to damage the rootball in the process.

3 Then add trailing lobelia to fill the rest of the space. The blue of the lobelias will form a vibrant contrast to the deep red of the begonias, and both colors will be set off by the warm tones of the terracotta container.

Canary creeper
(Tropaeolum peregrinum)

Coleus hybrid

French marigold
'Aurora'

Non-stop
begonia 'Rose'

Trailing lobelia
'Crystal Palace'

Above: Why not experiment with a new planting idea like this? The trick in mixing such brightly colored material is to choose flowers that 'pick out' one of the minor colors in the coleus leaves.

4 By midsummer you will hardly be able to see the container for the mass of flowers covering it. Be sure to water it often, as this type of porous terracotta container does not hold much soil and dries out quickly.

A formal display in a wire wall basket

Wall baskets are invariably rather narrow, so a fairly formal, symmetrical arrangement suits them best. A typical formal arrangement is based on a larger 'star' plant in the middle, with smaller supporting plants at the sides. Wire-framed wall baskets are particularly versatile, as you can plant into the sides as well as the top for a fuller display, as with a wire hanging basket. We have not done so here in order to keep the rounded shape of the basket. If you do decide to plant the sides and base, use slightly taller plants than shown here to balance out the trailing growth below, otherwise the basket will look a bit top-heavy. Adding trailing plants in the sides and base of the basket means that it will dry out twice as quickly as if you only planted the top. To create the impression of a fuller display, team several half-baskets together on the same stretch of wall. For a more interesting design, use a staggered row, rather than making a straight line. Or arrange them in a 'flight', with each one just below the level of the one ahead. For maximum effect, 'link' the display in the baskets with other containers or flowerbeds nearby. Or try a more mixed display, where the same plant or color appears in each basket, even if only in a small way.

3 *The centerpiece of this display is a cascading, or trailing, begonia that will tumble down over the sides of the basket. Deadhead it regularly to keep it flowering all summer.*

1 *This traditional style wire-framed wall basket needs lining before planting. There are special liners for 'half baskets. Alternatively, you could cut a piece of plastic to fit inside.*

2 *Fill the container almost to the rim with a good-quality soilless potting mix. This basket has a flat base, so you do not need to hang it up on the wall while you plant it.*

4 Create a symmetrical formal scheme by placing one ageratum on each side of the begonia. Knock them out of their pots and plant them without breaking the rootball.

6 When the basket is planted, water it thoroughly. This helps to settle the soil around the roots. If the soil level is too low, top it up to just below the rim of the container.

5 Silver foliage adds sparkle to an arrangement with a lot of similar-looking green leaves. Remove flowers that appear on foliage plants, as the leaves deteriorate once flowers develop.

Senecio bicolor (Cineraria maritima)

Floss flower (Ageratum)

Cascading begonia 'Finale'

7 Tuck in any flowers or foliage overhanging the back of the basket so they do not get trapped against the wall. Hang the finished container up on the wall.

Planting a trough of culinary herbs

Culinary herbs are always useful in the kitchen, but there is no reason why they should not look good in the garden, too. A trough of fresh herbs makes a most attractive feature by the kitchen door, where it is handy for picking. Herbs need a sheltered sunny spot to do well, so if your back door is not in the sun (or you use a lot of herbs) try having two troughs - one by the back door and the other where growing conditions are better - and switch them over regularly. When choosing herbs to plant, choose those you use most in cooking. Some of the best include those shown here, namely parsley, chives, rosemary, dill, sage and thyme. Colored-leaved varieties of popular herbs, such as tricolor and purple sage and variegated thyme, look better but taste just as good as the plain green ones. You could also add an unusual herb, such as the silver-leaved curry plant shown here. It looks attractive and really does smell and taste faintly of curry - try it in salads. Herbs are easy to care for. In a trough, they need regular feeding; you can use any good liquid feed, but those that contain seaweed improve flavor. Avoid overwatering. Herbs are fairly drought-resistant and would rather be slightly on the dry side than too wet.

1 Choose a terracotta trough measuring about 7x16in(18x40cm). Cover the drainage holes in the bottom with curved pieces of clean, broken clay pot, known as 'crocks'.

2 Cover the crocks with 1in(2.5cm) of grit. This allows surplus water to seep out of the drainage holes, but stops the potting mix washing out.

3 Fill the trough to within 2in(5cm) of the rim with good-quality soil-based potting mixture. Leave it loose and fluffy - do not firm it down.

Choose contrasting plants to put in next to each other. This is dill, which has feathery foliage that tastes faintly of aniseed.

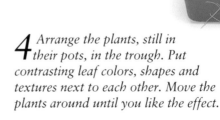

4 Arrange the plants, still in their pots, in the trough. Put contrasting leaf colors, shapes and textures next to each other. Move the plants around until you like the effect.

5 Lift all the plants out of the trough and then gently knock each one out of its pot ready for planting. If the plant does not slide out easily, give the pot a sharp tap on a hard surface to loosen it.

Thyme 'Silver Posie' is compact, variegated and edible. Use it in the same way as the normal plain green thyme.

Terracotta is porous, so plants dry out quickly - ideal for herbs, which dislike damp.

6 It is easiest to start planting from one end of the trough, as each plant holds the next in place. Stagger the position of alternate plants.

7 If the herbs came in round pots, there will be gaps between the rootballs where they do not quite fit together. Fill these spaces with a few extra handfuls of potting mixture.

8 Stand the completed trough in a sunny, sheltered spot and support it on pot 'feet' so that surplus water can run away easily. Water it thoroughly to settle the plants in.

Dill

Tricolor sage

Rosemary

Purple sage

Curry plant

Parsley

Chives

Thyme 'Silver Posie'

A miscellany of herb containers

Most of the popular culinary herbs, including chives, parsley and basil, as well as compact perennials, such as rosemary and thyme, grow well in containers. Clip them lightly after flowering to keep them compact and prune out any dead twigs in spring. Choose variegated or colored-leaved versions of everyday herbs, such as red basil or purple sage, for herbs that are both ornamental and useful. Feathery herbs, such as fennel or dill contrast well with more solid shapes. Mixing flowering herbs, such as feverfew and calendula (pot marigold), with culinary kinds improves the appearance of the group. Thymes and marjorams have very pretty flowers too, and attract butterflies and bees. To add more color still, old-fashioned cottage annuals associate well with herbs, and scented-leaved pelargoniums enjoy the same growing conditions. Invasive herbs, such as horseradish and apple mint, do well in separate containers of their own. Divide and repot them into fresh soil-based potting mix each spring - they quickly exhaust whatever they are growing in.

Right: A collection of culinary herbs in hand-painted pots on a kitchen windowsill. Keep some spare plants outdoors to replace those inside when they need a rest from being cut.

Below: This unusual shaped terracotta pot houses two kinds of thyme, tricolor sage, a dwarf lavender and houseleek, all of which have had herbal uses in the past. Houseleek was reputed to deter lightning!

Above: Variegated lemon balm has a strong lemon scent and looks stunning in a large pot. Trim shoots back to just above the top of the pot if they get too tall and flop over badly.

Below: *This well-planned group of edible herbs features variegated foliage, flowers and colored leaves. The two non-edible lobelias have been added to cascade down the front of the trough.*

Left: *Here, three terracotta pots have been placed one inside the other to show off the colors, shapes and textures of the mint collection planted in them.*

Climbers in containers

If wall space is limited, you can grow climbers up pergola poles and pillars or over arches. And if there does not happen to be any soil there, grow the climber in a container. Another good way of growing climbers, especially if you have a small garden, is on a framework that stands in the pot itself. 'Obelisks', such as the trellis shown here, are becoming very popular. This one is available ready made, packed flat, and can be assembled in minutes at home. Some climbers make good plants for containers. Of the annual climbers, plants such as canary creeper (*Tropaeolum peregrinum*), sweet peas, cup-and-saucer vine (*Cobaea scandens*), morning glory (*Ipomoea*), and Chilean glory vine (*Eccremocarpus*) are all good choices. But if you want a climber that can be left in the same container for several years at a time, a clematis is ideal.

All climbers in pots need generous feeding. Start two weeks after planting in the container, using a liquid or soluble tomato feed. This contains potash, which encourages flowering. After a few weeks, alternate this with a general-purpose feed.

Climbers also need frequent watering, especially when the container fills with roots, as the potting mixture dries out quickly at this stage. Although most annual climbers are real sun-lovers, clematis prefer cool conditions at the roots. In a sunny spot, stand other containers around them so that their foliage shades the soil and the base of the plant. Prune clematis in containers as if they were growing in the garden; pruning strategies vary from one variety to another, so keep the instructions that come on the back of the label when you buy the plant. After three years, tip the plant carefully out of its pot in early spring before it starts growing, carefully shake off the old soil and repot the clematis back into the same tub or one that is a size larger, using fresh potting mixture.

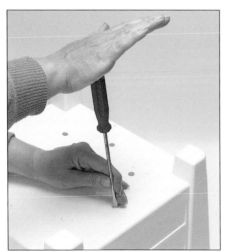

3 Fill the tub with a soil-based potting mix, leaving 1in(2.5cm) around the rim for watering. This still allows plenty of space for the rootball to develop.

4 Plant clematis deeper than they were planted in their original pots. Then if a plant suffers from clematis wilt, which kills the shoots, new ones can regrow from below the surface.

1 Plastic containers, such as this tub, have no holes in the base. Tap out the 'weak points' with a screwdriver if you want to use them outside.

2 Cover the drainage holes with 'crocks' - pieces of broken clay flowerpot - to stop the potting mix running out later on.

5 *Remove the cane that supports the plant when you buy it and separate the stems slightly. Arrange the trellis obelisk so that the legs stand firmly in the corners of the tub and press it down gently.*

6 *Space the stems evenly around the support frame and tie them loosely in place. If the plant is going to be seen mainly from one direction, make sure the plant's 'best side' faces front.*

7 *Water well in to settle the soil around the plant roots and the legs of the obelisk. If the soil sinks or the obelisk tips to one side, add more soil, adjust the obelisk and rewet the soil.*

8 *Most clematis prefer a coolish spot where the roots are in shade but the tops can grow into sunlight. Tie new growth in regularly to maintain a good shape, and remove dead flowers.*

Clematis 'Bees Jubilee'

A classic strawberry pot

Strawberries are both ornamental and productive in containers. If you do not have room for a conventional strawberry bed, a planter such as this is ideal, as you can pack plenty of plants into a very small space. For early strawberries, move the planter into a cold or slightly heated greenhouse in midwinter and the fruit will be ready to pick several weeks earlier than usual. Strawberry plants can be bought cheaply as young 'runners' in the fall or as pot-grown plants in the fall and spring. Continue planting even when the plants are in flower, but do not allow the roots to dry out. Most strawberries look pretty when flowering, but now you can obtain varieties with pink flowers instead of white ones. Some of these are intended to be mainly ornamental, with small strawberries as a bonus, but others give a good crop of fruit as well. Keep them well watered and feed every week with liquid tomato feed, from flowering time until after the crop has been picked.

Hold the rootball under the planting pocket and gently push the leafy top of the plant out through the hole.

3 Knock the plants out of their pots. The rootballs of pot-grown strawberries will be too big to fit into the planting pockets of the pot, so plant them from the inside. Secure the plants by firming the potting mix around the roots.

1 This pot has a very large drainage hole in the base, so instead of using a single crock, it is better to heap a small handful of crocks over it. These will help to keep the soil in the pot.

2 Fill the pot to 1in(2.5cm) below the bottom row of planting pockets in the side, using a soil-based potting mixture, which is heavy enough to keep the pot stable.

4 As you complete each layer of plants, top the container up with more potting mixture to just below the base of the next row of planting pockets until you reach the rim of the pot. Firm the soil gently down around the plant roots.

5 Depending on the size of the container, plant two or three strawberry plants in the top of the pot so that it is well filled. Use a little more potting mixture to fill any gaps between the plants.

6 Water the plants thoroughly and very slowly, so that the moisture soaks in and does not run out through the planting holes.

'Serenata' has pink flowers and a useful crop of fruit.

7 Position the completed planter in a sheltered, sunny spot and feed and water it regularly. Replace the potting mix and the plants every two or three years to keep the container productive.

Trim off the runners to encourage the parent plants to fruit.

Planting a fruit bush

If you do not have room for a proper fruit garden, it is perfectly feasible to grow a few plants in containers. Fruit trees, soft fruit bushes and strawberries are all good subjects. However, cane fruits are unsuitable, so avoid blackberries, loganberries, raspberries, etc. This is partly due to their size and because they need a strong support system, but they do not thrive for long in containers even if these problems can be overcome. Soft fruit bushes - red and white currants, and smaller varieties of blackcurrant and gooseberries - are particularly suitable subjects for pots. They are naturally compact and provide interest over a long season, starting with blossom in spring, developing fruit to watch in early summer and ripe fruit to enjoy in midsummer. Even after the fruit has been picked, the plants have pleasant, often faintly aromatic foliage, which makes a good 'foil' for colorful flowering plants in other containers. Fruit bushes do not need any kind of support and the ripening fruit is relatively easy to protect from birds if the plants are grown close to the house.

As the bushes will stay in the same pot for several years at a time, plant them into a good soil-based mixture. Keep them well watered; the soil should never dry out completely, particularly in summer, when the bushes are carrying their crop of fruit. At this time, they need more water than usual to help swell the fruit. If the roots dry out severely, the fruit will fall off. Fruit bushes in pots also need feeding frequently. A high-potash liquid feed is best, as fruit bushes use a lot of this particular nutrient. Apply a liquid tomato feed, diluted at the rate recommended for feeding tomatoes, every week from the time the leaves open in spring until late summer. Prune the plants in winter, in exactly the same way as you would if the plants were growing in the open ground. Every two to three years, knock the plants carefully out of their pots in early spring, shake the old soil from the roots and trim them slightly, and repot with fresh potting mix back into the same pot or one a size larger.

3 Carefully snip open film plastic pots and then pull them off. If the plant is in a rigid plastic pot, knock it gently out without breaking the rootball.

1 Choose a clay or plastic pot measuring at least 12in(30cm) in diameter, ideally 14-15in (36-38cm), but not so large that you cannot move it once it is full of soil. Cover the drainage hole with a concave 'crock'.

2 Partly fill the pot with a good soil-based potting mixture. Leave enough room for the rootball; check the depth by standing the plant, still in its pot, inside the new container and allowing one extra inch.

4 If the roots are coiled thickly round the base of the rootball, gently tease a few of the biggest ones out from the mass. If not pot-bound, do not break the rootball up. To plant, sit the fruit bush in the center of the new pot.

6 Finally, water in. Soft fruit bushes are heavy feeders, so start feeding them after the first week, using diluted tomato feed.

White currant 'White Dutch'

5 Fill the gap around the edge with more potting mix, barely covering the surface of the rootball. Leave a 1in(2.5cm) gap round the rim for watering later on.

Setting up a vegetable garden in containers

When there is no room for a vegetable plot, why not grow a selection of vegetables and salads in containers? Some kinds are very decorative when grown in this way. Good choices include tomatoes, peppers, eggplants, cucumbers, climbing and dwarf beans, edible podded peas and lettuce, all of which are productive and pretty.

Choose outdoor varieties of tomato that ripen well, even in cooler conditions. Modern varieties of outdoor cucumber look and taste like the greenhouse types (which do not do well out of doors). Vegetables that are normally grown in glasshouses, such as peppers and eggplants, need a very warm, sunny, sheltered spot to do well, though any edibles in containers need sun for at least half the day. Plant into a good soil-based mixture, and keep crops well watered and regularly fed. If the soil is allowed to dry out, the crops tend to develop problems. Lettuce may bolt; runner beans fail to set, and tomatoes can develop unsightly circles of black tissue at the end furthest from the stalk. As for feeding, this should begin one to two weeks after planting. Apply liquid or soluble feeds at least once a week from then on, but follow the manufacturer's directions. Give tomatoes, peppers and eggplants diluted tomato feed. Leafy crops and beans do best on a general-purpose feed.

3 Plant crops that grow in rows, such as lettuce, in a trough. Choose large individual pots for 'specimen' crops, such as tomatoes.

1 Choose large clay or plastic containers in a range of shapes and sizes to create an interesting, varied, edible plant arrangement.

2 Fill the containers to within 1in (2.5cm) of the rim with good-quality soil-based potting mix. They will be heavy once filled; stand them in their final position before beginning.

5 Plant runner beans around the edge of a wide container; if you have a few plants left over, plant them in a circle in the middle of the tub. Choose healthy, undamaged plants.

Outdoor tomato 'Alicante'

4 You put the plants more closely together than if they were in the garden as they are growing in richer soil - it is, in fact, potting mix - and they will be receiving more intensive care.

Space runner beans 6-8in (15-20cm) apart.

Space 'Little Gem' lettuces 6in(15cm) apart.

Vegetables all set to grow

2 *For climbing beans, tie the tops of the canes together above the center of the tub to form a strong 'wigwam'.*

Bush varieties of tomato are convenient to grow in containers as they are naturally compact, but if you prefer tall, upright varieties, nip out the growing tip of the plant after four clusters of flowers have formed. By 'stopping' the plants, you encourage the development of the fruit. You can help tomatoes and runner bean flowers to 'set' by spraying the plants and flowers with water daily from the time the first blooms open. 'Cut and come again' varieties of lettuce, such as the frilly 'Lollo Rosso', are very practical crops for containers. Pick a few leaves at a time and leave the plants growing. For flavor, choose the miniature cos lettuce 'Little Gem' and pick the whole lettuce when it forms a tight heart.

1 *After planting, give tall crops, such as tomatoes and runner beans, a cane each for support. Push these carefully in alongside each plant and about 2in(5cm) away.*

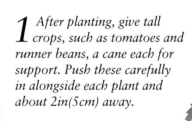

Above: Keep edible crops in hanging baskets well watered. Here two kinds of 'cut and come again' frilly lettuce are growing with a dwarf bush tomato - a salad at the door!

Remove these side shoots.

3 Tie tomatoes loosely to their canes to keep them upright. Add extra ties as the plants grow taller. All except bush varieties must have their sideshoots rubbed out too - these grow in the angle the leaf makes with the stem.

5 Regularly feed all vegetables in containers with liquid or soluble feeds to keep them growing fast - they will crop much better this way.

Tomato 'Alicante' produces a heavy crop of medium-sized, round, red fruit, with good flavor. Ideal for beginners.

Runner bean 'Streamline' is a reliable, well-flavored variety, with a heavy crop of pods 15-18in(38-45cm) long.

4 Water vegetables in thoroughly after planting and then make sure the soil never completely dries out, otherwise problems will soon develop.

'Little Gem' is probably the best-tasting lettuce ever developed. It is all heart and grows to about 8in(20cm) high.

Experimenting with tubs

Below: The head of David shown here is hollow and used as a container for potted plants that change from season to season. There are plenty of possibilities: try some grassy plants, such as Festuca, or trailing ones, such as Aubretia, for a touch of whimsy.

By the time you have used containers in all the usual places and tried all the popular combinations of plants and pots, you may fancy experimenting further. Why not look at some of the ways fellow container gardening enthusiasts have found to develop their ideas? Try to visit as many public and, where possible, private gardens for inspiration. You need not restrict yourself to what is normally grown in containers. Look out for whatever is new and interesting in nurseries, garden centers and seed catalogs and give them a try. Get to know a good circle of gardening acquaintances, share their experiences and swap surplus seedlings and cuttings with them to get new plants for free. And do try different combinations of plants and containers together. By now you will have discovered techniques to tell at a glance what will work and what will not. Here are a few ideas to be going on with.

Above: This 'potted pond' in a barrel has been sunk to just below the rim into the gravel to make it in scale with the plants around it. The rim prevents gravel being kicked into the water.

Right: A terracotta jar fitted with a submersible pump. The moving water adds a sparkle in a patch of waterside plants. A safe way of using water in a garden where there are small children.

Left: *A wooden dinghy makes a splendid container. To prevent the wood rotting, stand the pots on an unperforated plastic liner or use containers without holes in the base and water them with extra care.*

Below: *Make the best use of space by banking up containers in several tiers, using existing features, such as low walls, or on staging. Adding outdoor ornaments makes for a busier display.*

Decorating with containers

Below: A pair of matching trimmed topiary trees standing on either side of a doorway looks stunning in a formal setting. These are box, which needs clipping about four times a year to keep it looking neat. Box thrives in sheltered conditions and tolerates shade, so long as it regularly gets two hours of sun.

Containers can be used in all sorts of gardens, whether formal or informal, and can house plants of all kinds, from flowers and climbers to shrubs, vegetables and fruit. You can even grow topiary trees in pots. If space is short - for instance in a tiny town front garden - you can create a complete garden of containers and simply change the plants whenever they are past their best to keep the display looking fresh. (If there is space at the back, keep spare plants there until needed or even raise them from seed and cuttings). Use containers to turn balconies, flat roofs and concrete yards into productive gardening space. In large gardens, containers are useful close to the house or for accenting features within the garden. Move them around occasionally to give the garden an instant new look. And replant weatherproof containers with seasonal flowers to keep them filled with color all through the year.

Right: You can create a cottage garden look by growing flowers and vegetables in a suitable container. In this display, nasturtiums, marigolds (Tagetes) and red cabbage are teamed together in a natural wooden trough. Other colored vegetables make good container plants, too. Try purple dwarf beans, kohl rabi 'Purple Vienna' and golden zucchini for an eye-catching and edible arrangement. An added bonus is that they taste even better than the plain green varieties.

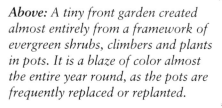

Above: *A tiny front garden created almost entirely from a framework of evergreen shrubs, climbers and plants in pots. It is a blaze of color almost the entire year round, as the pots are frequently replaced or replanted.*

Left: *Three pots of white primroses make a simple but effective display in an ornate container. As a general rule, the fancier the container, the simpler the planting should be to avoid ending up with an over-fussy result.*

Right: *The ultimate excuse for not digging the garden! Leaky boots, old shoes and wooden clogs can all be recycled as novelty plant containers. Try them standing on the doorstep, or hanging them up from a bracket. Do not be afraid to experiment!*

Index to Plants

Page numbers in **bold** indicate major text references. Page numbers in *italics* indicate captions and annotations to photographs. Other text entries are shown in normal type.

Credits

The majority of the photographs featured in this book have been taken by
Neil Sutherland and are © Colour Library Books. The publishers wish to
thank the following photographers for providing additional photographs,
credited here by page number and position on the page, i.e. (B)Bottom,
(T)Top, (C)Center, (BL)Bottom left, etc.

Eric Crichton: 53(BL)

John Glover: Half-title, 8, 10, 27(TR,L), 38-39, 42-43, 50-51, 53(BL),
55(C), 64-5, 78-79, 90(BL), 90-91(T), 91(BL), 100(BR), 102-103, 104-105

Harry Smith Photographic Collection: 55(B)

Acknowledgments

The publishers would like to thank Russell's Garden Center, near Chichester,
Sussex for providing facilities for location photography. Thanks are also due
to Country Gardens Alfold, near Cranleigh, Surrey for providing plants and
containers for photography.